Also by Tom Lacalamita

The Ultimate Bread Machine Cookbook
The Ultimate Pasta Machine Cookbook
The Ultimate Espresso Machine Cookbook
The Ultimate Pressure Cooker Cookbook

The All-New Ultimate Bread Machine Cookbook

101 BRAND-NEW, IRRESISTIBLE, FOOLPROOF RECIPES FOR FAMILY AND FRIENDS

TOM LACALAMITA

A FIRESIDE BOOK
PUBLISHED BY SIMON & SCHUSTER

FIRESIDE
Rockefeller Center
1230 Avenue of the Americas
New York, NY 10020

FIRESIDE and colophon are registered trademarks
of Simon & Schuster Inc.

Designed by Vertigo Design

Manufactured in the United States of America

10   9   8   7   6   5   4   3   2

Library of Congress Cataloging-in-Publication Data

Lacalamita, Tom.
     The all-new ultimate bread machine cookbook :
 101 brand-new, irresistible, foolproof recipes for family
 and friends / Tom Lacalamita.
         p.   cm.
     "A Fireside book."
     1. Bread.   2. Automatic bread machines.   I. Title.
 TX769.L235   1999   99-31352
 641.8' 15—dc21   CIP

ISBN 0-684-85528-3

For Yayi and Cristina

Acknowledgments

Special thanks to my editor, Syd Miner, for the opportunity to do this book, and for taking it through the evolution from manuscript to book. My thanks also to the rest of the Simon & Schuster team, Philip Metcalf, Jim Thiel, and Gabriel Levine, for their respective contributions along the path of this book's development.

Also to Brian Hagiwara for the beautiful portrayal of the breads on film, and to Tom Matt. Thanks also to Jackie Aher for the skillful illustrations.

When I undertook this project, I realized that I was both older and wiser since I had written my first bread machine cookbook, and would not have the same level of stamina that would enable me to deal with up to twenty bread machines demanding my attention at the same time, at least three times a day, during six months of recipe testing. With this in mind, I called upon my good friend and cohort Glenna Vance, who has worked with me on my other four cookbooks, to once again lend a hand or two, as well as her kitchen, dining room, and living room, to be my recipe tester and consultant *extraordinaire*. My hat goes off to this remarkable woman known by all for her extreme patience, dedication, and loyalty.

My sincere appreciation goes to all the manufacturers credited on page 197 for providing the equipment and ingredients needed in developing this book.

And, most important, thanks to my family and friends, for sharing with me my love of food, and for the knowledge and skills they have so graciously extended to me over the years.

Contents

Part One
Introduction
1. Bread Machines: East Meets West 15
  Who Uses a Bread Machine? 16
  Bread: The Key to a More Healthful Diet 17
  Why a Bread Machine? 18
  Kids and Bread Machines 19
2. Getting the Best Results from Your Bread Machine 21
  What Flour to Use? 22
  Active Dry, Fast Rising, or Bread Machine Yeast? 23
  Liquids: The Ingredients That Make It All Come Together 25
  Fat in Bread 26
  Sugar and Salt 26
  Fruit, Nuts, and Other Ingredients 27
  Measuring 101 27
  How Does a Bread Machine Work? 28
  Working with Dough 29
  Storing and Freezing Bread and Dough 31
  Gluten-Free Baking 31
  Problem Solving 32
  Getting Started 32
Part Two
Recipes
1. White-Bread Crowd Pleasers 35
  Homey White Bread 36
  Old-Fashioned Buttermilk White 38
  Real Farmhouse Potato Bread 39
  Chocolatey Walnut-Brownie Bread 41
  Cinnamon-Raisin Bread 42
  Cornmeal Honey Loaf 43
  Irish Freckle Bread 44

Old-Fashioned Oat Bread 45
Sourdough Starter 47
Sourdough White Bread 48
Salt-Rising Bread Starter 49
Salt-Rising Bread 50
Basic Chinese Bun Dough 51
Steamed Barbecued-Pork Buns 52
Buddha's Delightful Veggie Buns 53

2. Golden Egg Breads 54
Savory Egg Bread 55
Onion-Poppy-Seed Bread 57
Fresh Herb Bread 58
Sweet Bread 59
Orange-Cranberry-Walnut Loaf 61
Pumpkin-Pecan Bread 62
Glazed Lemon Poppy-Seed Loaf 63
Sweet Almond-and-Cherry Bread 65
Challah 66
Basic Dinner-Roll Dough 68
Parker House Rolls 69
Fan-Shaped Rolls 71
Cloverleaf Rolls 73
Herb-and-Cheese Rolls 75
Suizos 76
Pandoro 78
Basic Pull-Apart Bubble Bread Sweet Dough 80
Funny as a Monkey Chocolate-Crumb Pull-Apart Bread 81
Apple-Chunk and Walnut Pull-Apart Bread 82
Tropical Hawaiian Bubble Bread 83

3. Whole-Grain Goodness 84
Golden Wheat Bread 85
Wheat-Flake Potato Bread 87
Banana-Raisin Oat Bread 89
PBJ (Peanut-Butter-and-Jelly) Bread 91
Multigrain Bread 92
100 Percent Whole-Wheat Bread 93
Apple-Walnut Wheat Bread 94
Whole-Wheat Date-Nut Bread 95
Basic Whole-Wheat Pastry Dough 96

Sweet or Savory Butterhorns 97
Coconut-Pecan Coffee Cake 99

4. Spanning the Globe with Rye Bread 101
Good Old New York Deli Rye 102
Swedish *Limpa* Rye 103
St. Paddy's Day Rye 105
Rye Sour Starter 106
Old Milwaukee Sourdough Rye Bread 107
Russian Black Bread 108
Pumpernickel Roll-Up Sandwich 110

5. Breads with a Flair 112
Basic European White Bread 113
Semolina Bread with Toasted Sesame Seeds 114
Black-Olive-and-Rosemary Bread 115
Chewy Country Bread with Seeds 116
Tomato-and-Basil Bread 117
Pesto-and-Toasted-Walnut Bread 118
French Bread 119
Banneton 121
Partybrot 123
Dutch-Crunch Dinner Rolls 125

6. Just Like from the Pastry Shop 127
Classic *Brioche* Dough 128
Brioches à Tête 130
Sticky Buns 132
Danish *Kringle* 134
The World's Best Jelly Doughnuts 136
Raised Doughnuts and Doughnut Holes 138
Christmas *Stollen* 140
Fresh Fruit *Kuchen* 142
Crumb Buns 144
Quick-and-Easy Holiday Breads 146
Christmas Trees 147
Valentine Hearts 148
St. Paddy's Day Shamrocks 149
Easter Bunnies 150

7. Pizza and Flat Breads 151
Traditional Thin Pizza Crust 152
Classic Tomato-and-Cheese Pie 153

White Pizza 155
South-of-the-Border Pizza 156
Chicago Deep-Dish Pizza 157
Deep-Dish Taco Bake 159
Garlic Knots 161
Calzone 164
Basic *Focaccia* 166
Onion-and-Sage *Focaccia* 168
Greek Flat Bread 170
Aladdin's Bread 172

8. Pushcart Breads 174
Basic Bagel and Pretzel Dough 175
Basic Chewy New York–Style Bagels 176
Real German–Style Pretzels 178
Butter-Dipped Pretzels 180
Potato Knishes 181

9. Great Things to Make with Leftover Bread 183
Cinnamon Toast 184
Bread-Pudding Pancakes 185
Caramel-Apple Bread Pudding 186
Strata 188
Tomato and Bread 189
Panzanella 190
Salmorejo 191

Troubleshooting 192
Bread Machine and Ingredient Manufacturers 197
Mail-Order Sources 199
Index 201

PART ONE

INTRODUCTION

AUTOMATIC BREAD MACHINES, ONE OF THE MOST POPULAR home appliances to be introduced in years, were originally developed in Japan for Japanese consumers. Although rice has been, and remains, the staple starch in the Japanese diet, bread boutiques and specialty bakeries with European-sounding names began popping up all over Japan in the 1970s, as Japan began to experience an economic boom. Young Japanese were finding the Western breakfast of bacon and eggs with orange juice and bread and rolls to be more convenient and to their

Bread Machines:
East Meets West

liking than a bowl of rice porridge with pickled vegetables. Unfortunately for the Japanese housewife, her family only likes very fresh bread, so she has to get up early to go out every morning to buy the family's breakfast bread. That was true until electrical engineer Shin Ojima was finally able to manufacture his invention, a totally automatic bread machine. After many false starts, Ojima had convinced a Japanese appliance manufacturer of the merits of this revolutionary appliance, and the first automatic bread machine appeared in Japan in 1987.

Even at prices exceeding four hundred dollars, automatic bread machine sales took off, and more than 1 million units were sold in less than twelve months. This success was to be short-lived since, within a year, the bottom fell out. Most Japanese live in very small apartments that have sliding, paper-covered partitions for walls. Since most people wanted to have their bread ready in the morning, they would place the ingredients in the bread machine, and set the programmable timer before going to bed in order to have a loaf of fresh, hot bread waiting for them when they awoke. Well, imagine trying to sleep cuddled up to a bread machine. Between the noise and aroma, many Japanese families found it difficult to sleep and, thus, abandoned the idea of homemade bread by putting the machines out with the trash. Fortunately for Japanese manufacturers, the United States and Canada presented a large, untapped market, ready and waiting for such an appliance.

The first bread machines reached North America in time for Christmas 1988. Originally retailing for more than $400, they have since dropped in price dramatically, while the demand has risen steadily, affording millions of people the opportunity to make delicious, wholesome bread with the push of a button.

Who Uses a Bread Machine?

Early on, the average bread machine purchaser was fifty-five to sixty-five years old, and somewhat affluent. They were financial risk takers, who had the expendable income to purchase the latest and newest gadgets on the market. With the downsizing of corporate America at the beginning of the nineties we also saw many men from this age group, forced out of the work force with incentive retirement packages, picking up bread machine baking as a hobby or as an introduction to cooking.

Since their introduction over ten years ago, bread-machine retail prices have dropped to under one hundred dollars, which has initiated a change in who uses them. For the most part, today's consumer is a thirty- to thirty-nine-year-old married woman, with children, who works outside the home. The bread machine allows her to make homemade loaves of bread for brown-bag lunches, or to supplement prepared takeout meals from the local supermarket or fast-food restaurant with a wholesome loaf of homemade bread.

Bread: The Key to a More Healthful Diet

In 1992, after many years of research and planning, the U.S. government redefined the four basic food groups and introduced the Food Pyramid. Complex carbohydrates, which consist of grains and cereals, are now the foundation of the pyramid. After years of being told that complex carbohydrates were high in calories, we are now advised that, in order to lower the incidence of serious illnesses like cancer, heart disease, and diabetes, we should increase our consumption of complex carbohydrates by 50 percent, and substantially reduce the amount of animal protein, fats, and sugar in our diet.

Even in light of all the documented studies, obesity, which can lead to hypertension, is presently a national crisis. In 1997, an eating plan from the Dietary Approaches to Stop Hypertension clinical study (DASH) was released. Funded by units of the National Institutes of Health, the DASH diet, similar to the Food Guide Pyramid, also recommends that the bulk of our diet come from grains and grain products (at least seven to eight servings a day), with reduced intake of meats, poultry, and fish. The study also recommends an increase in foods rich in sources of iron, magnesium, potassium, protein, and fiber.

After years of a meat-and-potatoes diet and, more recently, that of fast food, eaten by so many young Americans, we are faced with the dilemma of learning how to increase our intake of carbohydrates and, at the same time, maintain an appetizing diet. That's where your bread machines comes in handy.

Since bread derives at least 60 percent of its calories from carbohydrates, it is a healthful, filling food product, usually low in fat and cholesterol and should be a fundamental part of every diet. By using your automatic bread machine, you can make an endless variety of healthful and nutritious breads for yourself, your family, and your friends.

The diverse and varied recipes in this book are designed to have a broad appeal, with everyone in mind. There are recipes that contain zero milligrams of cholesterol, with fat limited to only that contained in the flour. While other recipes, like *brioche,* are substantially higher in fat and cholesterol, they are still surprisingly lower in fat than other baked goods like cakes, pies, and pastries. Nevertheless, the key to a well-balanced diet is variety and moderation.

Why a Bread Machine?

For hundreds of years, housewives were responsible for baking their family's daily bread. It was a ritual that took at least two days: one day to make the dough and heat the wood-burning oven, and the next to bake the risen loaves. The process was labor intensive, performed exclusively by hand and took from early morning to late in the day. Naturally, enough bread was baked at one time to last a week. The industrial revolution in the late 1800's, a shift in society from a rural to a more urban lifestyle, dictated a change in cooking and eating practices. Bread baking started to become more commercial, with city dwellers buying bread on a daily basis from their neighborhood bakery. Home baking became a hobby rather than a necessity, with a cherished recipe from the old country prepared on occasion for holidays or special events.

Over the course of time, home bread baking declined even further as more women entered the work force and scratch cooking took a back seat to prepared foods and baked goods.

When bread machines were first introduced, it would have been anyone's guess what kind of popularity they would achieve. Even though nothing could be more simple than carefully measuring ingredients and pushing a button, why would people want to spend time and money on a machine to make bread when they could buy acceptable, if not very good, bread at their local supermarket or bakery? With total sales over 20 million, it is obvious that the bread machine has been well received. At the risk of oversimplifying the reasons, we can easily assume that in this fast-paced world of late meetings, soccer practice, and dance classes, all of which cut into family time, a loaf of homemade bread baking on the counter in a bread machine sort of makes sense of it all. It is the homemade aspect of it that makes life a bit more manageable, if not better. Even if the chicken is hot off the rotisserie from the supermarket, the veggies zapped for three minutes in the microwave, and the salad prewashed and out of a plastic bag, the intoxicating smell of baking bread signifies *home* and all the traditional values that go with it. And if that is what it takes to sustain us, then why not?

Kids and Bread Machines

Have you ever met a child who wasn't curious? Probably not. In fact, today's children are usually computer literate before they even start kindergarten. They are attracted to everything that has buttons and lights, and instinctively seem to know which to push, and when. Since a bread machine is nothing more than a mixer and oven with a built-in computer, it is a natural for children, when used with adult supervision. Kids, as we all know, also love to touch and get their hands into things. I cannot think of a better project or activity than to make something good to eat; that's where your bread machine comes in.

Studies have shown that, while academic excellence often relies on committing facts to memory, parents should encourage their children in the creative application of information. Allowing children to participate in baking activities at an early age sets the stage for constructive learning.

Preschoolers can learn self-help skills, such as picking and measuring ingredients, and learn to take turns and think collectively rather than individually. Other acquired skills include fine-motor-skill development and eye-to-hand coordination, as well as a number of thinking, social, and emotional skills, and, ultimately, the fun, pride and satisfaction of eating their own creations made with mom or dad.

Bread-machine use can also reinforce newly acquired math and science skills when elementary school children measure ingredients using ounces and fractional components of measuring. Since bread baking is a chemical reaction, their inquisitive minds will enjoy viewing the process and transformation from ingredients, to dough, to bread.

By the time children reach middle or high school, they are ready to assume more family responsibilities. In fact, a recent Rand Youth Poll showed that 61 percent of teenagers polled cooked a meal at least once a week, while 49 percent went food shopping. Adolescents are becoming more involved in the meal process—planning, purchasing, and preparation. They are also looking for convenience and quickness. Baking in a bread machine teaches them valuable work skills, such as time allocation, planning, following directions, reasoning, and decision making. It also enhances personal qualities, such as self-esteem, when the finished loaf of bread or homemade pizza is served to family and friends. The best part is that all they have to do is measure carefully and push a button.

AS AN AVID BREAD BAKER, COOKBOOK AUTHOR, AND housewares consultant I have used at least 100 different bread machines during the past ten years to make thousands of loaves of bread, not to mention endless numbers of pizzas, cinnamon rolls, bread sticks, and so on. What never ceases to amaze me is how easy it is to get excellent results with a minimum of effort.

While making bread in a bread machine could not be easier, there are numerous variables that can affect how the bread comes out, regardless of whether you are making it by hand or

Getting the Best Results from Your Bread Machine

with an appliance. The most important thing to understand is how the different ingredients work together. Basically, bread is nothing more than flour, yeast, and water. Simple, right? Well, it's amazing how something so simple can go wrong so easily.

What Flour to Use? The next time you go to the supermarket, look at how many different types of flour are on the shelf. You'll find unbleached and bleached, all-purpose flour, self-rising flour, cake flour, soft flour for biscuits, whole-wheat flour, instant flour, rye flour, buckwheat, and lastly, and, perhaps the newest addition to the lineup, bread flour. All these flours, with the exception of rye and buckwheat, are milled from wheat. Pretty simple and straightforward right? Well, not really. With the exception of bread flour, none of the other flours will give you good results when making bread in a bread machine.

Wheat and some other grains contain a natural protein called *gluten*. When mixed with liquid, the gluten develops a network of elastic-like strands that allow the dough to stretch and trap the gases produced by the yeast. As the dough is kneaded, the gluten network continues to develop and strengthen, allowing the dough to support the weight and shape of the bread. The more gluten the flour has, the more stretching the dough can do and, naturally, the better the loaf of bread. High-gluten flour also absorbs liquid better than other flour and, since bread is over 30 percent liquid, this is important to bear in mind.

All wheat, however, is not created equal. Flour milled from hard, or winter wheat has the highest gluten content, and is sold in five-pound bags as bread flour. This higher gluten content is what gives bread its distinct, chewy texture.

Flours milled and sold for making cakes, biscuits, and pastries are made with spring, or soft wheat, which has a much lower gluten content, allowing for a softer crumb and texture.

When you blend approximately 80 percent hard wheat with 20 percent soft you come up with all-purpose flour. When the flour is aged naturally to bleach out the natural yellow pigment present in freshly milled flour, it is called *unbleached.* Bleached all-purpose flour is aged quickly with chlorine dioxide. All-purpose flour provides satisfactory results when baking cookies, quick breads, most cakes, and even yeast bread, when kneaded by hand. However, since a bread machine kneads more vigorously than we can with our hands, the gluten can break down and the dough not rise as needed. Therefore, unless specified otherwise, always use bread flour when using your bread machine.

Whole-wheat, or graham flour is ground from the entire wheat kernel. Because whole-wheat flour is not as refined as white bread flour, the bread made from it, while having a distinctive nutty flavor, may not rise as high and can have a denser texture. To overcome this, try to find whole-wheat bread flour, available at health food or specialty food retailers, or, for best results, use a combination of white bread flour and whole-wheat flour.

Keep in mind that, since wheat is organic, the quality of the crop can vary from harvest to harvest. While the flour mills blend different types of wheat to maintain certain standards and levels of protein (gluten) and moisture, variations can occur, which will affect how the flour performs. You may find that all of a sudden your tried-and-true white-bread recipe is not coming out as it had before. What you may be experiencing is that the wheat, due to poor growing conditions, has a lower gluten content or a higher moisture content. Perhaps you should try another brand of flour, or try "strengthening" the dough by adding a dough conditioner, available through some mail-order catalogs (see page 199). Dough conditioners usually contain all-natural ingredients, such as ascorbic acid (vitamin C), dried whey, malt powder, and vegetable gluten. They help to fortify the dough so that it rises better. Two homemade remedies are adding a teaspoon or two of lemon juice and/or a couple of tablespoons of rye flour to the ingredients. These two "fixes" provide excellent results when you experience minor trouble, such as collapsing or wrinkled loaves.

Other popular flours used in bread baking are semolina, rye, and buckwheat. *Semolina flour* is milled from a type of hard wheat called *durum*. It has a very distinct golden color and can have great elasticity; however, semolina has less than ideal liquid-absorption properties when it comes to making bread, and should be blended with bread flour for best results.

Rye, a grain valued for generations for its heartiness, is very low in gluten and must always be combined with bread flour. *Buckwheat,* surprisingly enough, is not a wheat nor is it a grain. Rather it is milled from the seeds of the buckwheat plant and, therefore, contains no gluten, whatsoever. Nevertheless, a few spoonfuls added to a loaf of bread makes a nice change.

Active Dry, Fast Rising, or Bread Machine Yeast?

Yeast, regardless of type, is the ingredient that causes dough to rise. It is a single-cell organism or plant that grows and multiplies as it ferments sugar. The fermentation process produces ethyl alcohol and carbon dioxide. The gases are trapped in the dough in the form of small bubbles, which then force the dough to rise.

Used since the days of the ancient Egyptians to make bread and fermented beverages, 99 percent of the consumer yeast used today is sold in dried, granular particles. This yeast starts out like the compressed cake yeast of days gone by, the difference being that it is baked until bone dry, and then crushed to form small particles. This form of yeast is dormant when purchased, and has a shelf life of approximately twelve months. To activate it, mix it with warm water.

Over the years, yeast companies have been developing and selecting different strains of yeast to provide the home bread baker with an easy-to-use product that gives consistent baking results. When purchasing yeast, you can choose between active dry, fast-rising, or bread-machine types, all of which can be used in a bread machine. The recipes in this cookbook generically specify *dry yeast*. I recommend that when purchasing yeast, you carefully read the manufacturer's package information to determine proper suitability for bread machine bread baking. You may also wish to experiment with different types of yeast to find the one that works best in your particular model bread machine.

Yeast is available at all supermarkets in three ¼-ounce packet strips or four-ounce jars. You can also purchase one- or two-pound packages at some warehouse clubs. When purchasing or using yeast, always check the expiration date. Yeast loses its activity as it gets closer to, or passes, the expiration date; it should then be discarded. Since yeast is very perishable when exposed to air, moisture, and/or warmth, all opened packages of yeast must be refrigerated in an airtight container. Under refrigeration, the life of yeast is about four months. Since your bread will rise less or not at all if using inactive yeast, check its activity if you have doubts. To do so, dissolve one teaspoon of sugar in ¼ cup of warm water (100 to 110 degrees) in a one-cup measuring cup. Stir in one packet or 2¼ teaspoons of dry yeast and let sit ten minutes. In three to four minutes, the yeast will have absorbed enough water to activate and will begin to rise to the surface. If at the end of ten minutes, the yeast has increased in volume and has a rounded crown, it is very active and may be used immediately in your bread machine. Just remember to deduct ¼ cup of liquid from the recipe to adjust for the water used in the test.

If there is no or limited activity, the mixture should be discarded and fresh yeast purchased.

When making bread by hand, the yeast is mixed with warm liquid, as discussed. If the liquid is hotter than 115 degrees, the yeast may be killed, and the bread will not rise. If cooler than 70 degrees, you run the risk of some or all of the yeast cells not activating, and the dough never rising. Since a bread machine efficiently mixes the ingredients, it is unnecessary to dissolve the yeast in water before adding it to the other ingredients (unless you wish to check on its viability). Since the dough is kneaded in an enclosed container, the friction created during kneading causes the dough temperature to rise substantially. Therefore, disregard the use instructions that come with the yeast and only use liquids that are approximately 70 to 80°F.

Liquids: The Ingredients That Make It All Come Together

Liquid ingredients play three important roles in breadmaking. First, they blend with the flour and other dry ingredients to form a soft mass, or dough. Second, they allow the gluten to develop the necessary elastic network of strands that will form the loaf, and, last, they rehydrate the dormant yeast so that it reactivates to start fermentation and the rising process.

Liquid ingredients can be much more than water or milk. They include eggs, honey, molasses, any type of fruit or vegetable purée, and liquid fats like oil and melted butter.

Let's start with water. All water is not treated equally, and I mean that literally. Drinking water is chemically treated, and certain chemicals can adversely affect the yeast. Chemically treated water high in fluoride and chlorine, for example, can slow down the rising process, resulting in low, stubby loaves, while well water can be another problem: Hard water can slow down the rising process and soft water can cause "sticky-dough syndrome." To remedy these problems, try using bottled water.

When bread machines first became available here, every single recipe seemed to contain nonfat dry milk. As far as I am able to determine, there is no logical reason, other than that the original bread machine recipes from Japan all contained nonfat dry milk. Since we all have liquid milk in the refrigerator, I have decided to simplify things and specify it when milk is called for in a recipe, therefore, eliminating the need for nonfat dry milk altogether. You can either use whole, low fat or fat-free milk. Milk gives bread a softer, ivory-colored crumb as opposed to just using water. Buttermilk on the other hand, makes bread moister, as does mashed potatoes and potato water.

Eggs add color and protein, and strengthen the dough. Always use extra-large eggs: they each provide approximately ¼ cup of liquid.

All liquids should be between 70 and 80 degrees when making bread in a bread machine. Water can be drawn straight from the tap; milk can be warmed in the microwave. To bring eggs to room temperature, place whole eggs in a bowl of warm water and let sit ten to fifteen minutes.

Fat in Bread

Fat has come to have a negative connotation in our food vocabulary; this is unfortunate since we need to consume some fat in order to be healthy. Many foods, including grains, contain some fat. That's why, for example, whole wheat flour turns rancid after a period of time. Nevertheless, fat in bread makes for a more tender, more flavorful loaf.

Fat, be it butter, margarine, shortening, or oil, coats the flour particles, so that elastic formation slows down; it makes the gluten strands slippery, so the gas bubbles can move easily, giving the bread finer texture. Tasteless oils like vegetable and seed oils and shortening do not affect the color or the taste of the bread. When a recipe calls for vegetable oil, I recommend making a healthy choice, such as canola. On the other hand, butter, margarine, and olive oil add flavor as well as golden color to the crumb.

Sugar and Salt

Besides enhancing bread flavor, sugar and salt help the yeast do its job. Remember, in order to ferment, yeast needs sugar. However, too much sweetener and the yeast produces large amounts of ethyl alcohol, inebriating itself along the way, slowing down the rising process. This is why sweet breads take longer to rise. Salt, on the other hand, acts to stabilize the dough by slowing down the rising action.

Other sweeteners besides sugar can be used interchangeably in making bread in your bread machine, including honey, molasses, maple syrup, and corn syrup. Bear in mind, however, that artificial sweeteners do not ferment and cannot be substituted for sugar.

Since flour contains a small percentage of natural sugar, bread can be made without any additional sugar. The dough will stop rising sooner, it will be less developed, and the resulting loaf will have a chewier crumb, as with most types of baguettes and flat breads, like pizza and focaccia. For best results, I recommend preparing bread without sugar only when the dough is going to be shaped by hand.

You can also prepare bread without salt if you are on a sodium-restricted diet. The dough, however, may rise unpredictably, and the resulting loaf may taste flat. That issue can be remedied by adding herbs or spices.

Fruit, Nuts, and Other Ingredients

The taste and look of a basic bread is easily changed or modified by adding ingredients like chopped dried fruits, nuts, cheese, spices, and herbs. Always add ingredients like dried fruit and nuts at the moment appropriate for your bread machine, or five minutes before the end of the last kneading cycle. Cheese, herbs, and spices can be added at the beginning, after the dry ingredients.

Measuring 101

Besides using the best-quality ingredients, it is essential that they be at room temperature and measured accurately. Bread baking, regardless of the method, is based on using a formula. If that formula is altered improperly, the results can and will be disappointing.

To measure accurately, be sure to use real measuring cups and spoons; coffee cups and soup spoons are not meant for measuring. Dry measuring cups and spoons do not have a lip, which allows you to level the ingredients off with the flat edge of a knife.

For measuring small amounts of dry ingredients like yeast, sugar, salt, herbs, and spices, sprinkle or scoop the ingredients into the measuring cup or spoon. Since it has a tendency to settle, never use the measuring cup to scoop flour, since you will most likely come up short. Flour should be spooned into the appropriate-size measuring cup, a spoonful at a time, until it mounds. Then, take the flat edge of a knife and run it along the edge of the measuring cup until the flour is level. Never pack the flour down.

For easy measuring of sticky sweeteners like honey and molasses, cover the measuring spoon with a light coating of oil. The sweetener will slide off without any trouble. Measuring butter, margarine, and shortening is easy since they can be purchased in premeasured sticks.

Liquid ingredients, like oil, water, and milk, should be measured using a glass or plastic measuring cup designed for measuring liquids. To use, place the cup on a level surface and fill to the appropriate measurement line at eye level.

I particularly like using a digital kitchen scale when measuring ingredients. Available at most housewares stores, you are able to measure ingredients directly in the bread machine pan by placing it on the scale, then adjusting the scale down to zero ounces. After weighing out the correct amount of water, for example, reset the scale back to zero, then weigh the flour. By measuring slowly, you can achieve accurate measurements while, at the same time, eliminating the need for various-size measuring cups. The following are some of the weight equivalents you will need to know if you should decide to use a scale.

	BREAD FLOUR	WHOLE-WHEAT FLOUR	SUGAR	WATER	MILK
1 tablespoon			½ oz.	½ oz.	½ oz.
¼ cup	1¼ oz.	1½ oz.	1¾ oz.	2 oz.	2¼ oz.
⅓ cup	1¾ oz.	2 oz.	2¼ oz.	2½ oz.	2¾ oz.
½ cup	2½ oz.	2¾ oz.	3½ oz	4 oz.	4½ oz.
⅔ cup	3¼ oz.	3¾ oz.	4½ oz.	5 oz.	5½ oz.
¾ cup	3¾ oz.	4 oz.	5¼ oz.	6 oz	6¼ oz.
1 cup	5 oz.	5½ oz.	7 oz.	8 oz.	8½ oz.

Nevertheless, regardless of the ingredient or the method of measuring, all ingredients should always be at room temperature in order for the yeast to activate properly, and for the dough to rise evenly.

How Does a Bread Machine Work?

The bread machine is the only appliance available for consumer use that can take basic ingredients and, with the push of a button, and no further human intervention, convert them into food automatically. Although the basic process is ages old, the method is most definitely based on twenty-first-century technology.

Bread machines are rated by the size loaf that they can make, and are available in a variety of sizes starting with one pound (small), one and a half pound (regular), two pounds (large), and two and a half pounds (extra-large). Most machines today can make different-sized loaves, usually one and a half and two pounds. The recipes in this book are for these two sizes, and are designated Regular (one and a half pounds) and Large (two pounds). The dough-only recipes are a standard size, and can be used in all machines one and a half pounds (regular), up to two and a half pounds (extra-large).

After carefully measuring the ingredients, adding them to the pan, and locking it in place, you then select the type of bread you are preparing, which, in turn, determines the cycle times. After *start* is pressed, most bread machines begin mixing and kneading the ingredients immediately, while others may have a preheating cycle to warm the ingredients to at least room temperature, if they are not warm enough. After the first kneading, the bread machine stops, and the dough rises while the program continues. At a pre-determined moment, the bread machine will knead for a second time, then rest for the final rise and shaping. After rising for a second time, the bread machine will automatically bake the dough into a golden loaf of bread.

Most bread machines include such basic features as a *delay-bake function,* which allows you to place the ingredients in the bread machine and set a timer that will delay the breadmaking process for up to twelve hours. This is great when you want to enjoy hot baked bread straight from the oven for breakfast, for example. Another important feature is the *dough-only program,* which does everything but bake the dough. This program is used for making yeast dough, which can be turned into, among other things, rolls or pizza which can then be baked in a regular oven.

Working with Dough

One of the greatest pleasures of owning a bread machine is being able to make an endless variety of hand-shaped breads. The machine does all of the work, while you take all the credit! The following are some guidelines to follow in order to achieve the best possible results.

Always remember to set the bread machine on the manual or dough setting when you plan to hand shape and bake using a conventional oven. Most bread machines finish the cycle with a partial rise, and mark the end of the cycle with a beeping sound.

While the dough is still in the pan, punch it down with your knuckles. Scoop the collapsed dough from the pan and place on the floured work surface. If sticky, sprinkle lightly with flour. Since the gluten is taut, let the dough rest a few minutes. If you find, when working yeast dough, that it keeps on springing back when stretched, let it sit a few minutes longer to allow the gluten to relax. Once the dough begins to cooperate, you can begin shaping it as specified in the recipe.

Place the shaped dough in or on the appropriate pan and cover with a clean kitchen cloth, so that the dough's surface does not dry out and form a hard, dry skin. The dough should rise in a warm (80 to 90 degrees), draft-free location until doubled in bulk. This can take anywhere from forty-five minutes to two hours, depending on the weather, the room temperature, and the type of dough. Sweet dough and doughs with greater fat content usually take longer to rise. You cannot and should not rush the rising process. If the dough does not rise sufficiently before being baked, the bread will be tough. The best way to determine that the dough has risen sufficiently is to perform the ripeness test. Lightly touch the shaped, risen dough with your finger tip. If an indentation remains, the dough has risen sufficiently and is ready to be baked.

Unless otherwise specified, yeast dough should be baked on the center rack of a preheated oven. Be sure to keep the oven door closed during the first few minutes, since the yeast dough goes through one final, very quick rise called *oven spring*. This is what gives many breads and baked goods that distinct, crowned look. If the bread browns too quickly, cover the top with a tented piece of foil.

Sometimes, when baking European-style bread, I will place a few ice cubes on the bottom of the oven, so that they create steam as they melt. The steam helps set the crust during the first few minutes of baking, making it chewier and harder.

The most accurate way to tell when the bread is done is by inserting an instant-read thermometer in the center of the bread. Instant-read thermometers are available at most housewares stores. When the thermometer registers 180 to 190 degrees, remove the bread from the oven and let cool on a wire rack to room temperature. Another way to check whether the bread is done is to tap the bottom of the baked loaf. If it has a hollow sound to it, it is most likely done.

Since yeast dough continues baking as it cools, do not cut the bread until it is cool enough to handle, pizza being the exception to the rule.

Storing and Freezing Bread and Dough

One of the greatest pleasures of home-baked bread, after that of the heavenly aroma, is that you control what goes into the loaf; all your breads will be free of artificial ingredients and preservatives. Home-made bread, however, has a limited shelf life—one to two days—when wrapped in plastic or foil. If you find yourself stockpiling bread, you can freeze it by wrapping it tightly in plastic or foil, then storing in an airtight plastic bag in the freezer for up to eight weeks. To defrost, remove from the plastic bag and let defrost at room temperature, partially unwrapped. Do not store bread in the refrigerator; it will dry out.

Yeast dough for pizza, rolls, and other uses can also be made beforehand and frozen up to one month. To do so, punch the dough down to deflate. Pat into a flat, one-inch-thick disk and place in an airtight plastic bag. Remove from the freezer and thaw overnight before using.

Gluten-Free Baking

After reading so much about the importance of using high-gluten wheat flour to achieve the best results, it may seem contradictory to talk about gluten-free baking. While wheat flour is necessary for making traditional breads and yeast doughs, there are hundreds of thousands of people worldwide who are allergic to the gluten found in wheat and other grains. Many of the individuals suffer from celiac sprue disease, which, although first reported in the first or second century, still remains without a cure. The best known way of living with the disease is by following a strict gluten-free diet. Naturally, all forms of bread and baked goods as we know them are restricted. However, thanks to the dedicated work of certain individuals and companies, people suffering from celiac sprue disease can now make a wide variety of breads and baked goods using a bread machine and gluten-free ingredients.

Celiacs can call toll-free at 1-800-4-CELIAC (1-800-423-

5422) to request a special brochure of gluten-free bread recipes or to speak to a home economist who can provide gluten-free baking assistance. Information is available twenty-four hours a day.

Bette Hagman, an author and lecturer who has celiac sprue disease, has written a series of highly acclaimed cookbooks of gluten-free recipes: *The Gluten-Free Gourmet, More from the Gluten-Free Gourmet,* and *Gluten-Free Gourmet Cooking, Fast and Healthy.* A new book of gluten-free bread recipes will be published in 1999. Besides being a valuable source of information on maintaining a gluten-free diet, these books also provide recipes for gluten-free breads and other baked goods that can be made with a bread machine.

Most gluten-free ingredients can be purchased at your local health-food store; I have included for your convenience two mail-order sources which can be found on page 199.

Problem Solving By following the instructions and guidelines provided in this book, you should be able to achieve excellent results with your bread machine. In the event you run into any problems or have any questions, refer to the chapter on troubleshooting, page 192. Nevertheless, before using your bread machine for the first time, you should read the owner's manual and all of the printed materials provided by the manufacturer in order to familiarize yourself with the operation of the appliance.

If you do run into problems and all else fails, bear in mind that all reputable manufacturers have a staff of trained product specialists who are available to assist you with any technical and baking questions that you may have. The larger ingredient companies that manufacture yeast and flour also have trained home economists to assist you with baking-related questions. A list of bread-machine manufacturers' customer-service phone numbers, as well as those for the major ingredient companies, can be found on pages 197 to 198.

Getting Started Congratulations! Now that you have read all of this information, you are ready to make your first loaf of bread. The following recipes are from my personal collection. Many are for breads and baked goods that I have eaten over the years and adapted for making in the bread machine for my family and friends. I sincerely hope that you will enjoy them as much as we do.

PART TWO

RECIPES

A GOOD PLACE TO START WHEN MAKING BREAD IS WITH the most basic of recipes, white bread. Much maligned over the years as being tasteless and all fluff, good white bread can be substantial and pleasing. It is also the basis for endless variations with the addition of fruits, nuts, spices, and herbs. The recipes in this chapter provide a broad sampling of white breads, from basic white to a very chocolatey, walnut brownie bread.

White bread flour is also an all-natural food product without any artificial preservatives. As required by U.S. law, it is for-

White-Bread Crowd Pleasers

tified and contains niacin, iron, thiamine, riboflavin, and folic acid. A good source of complex carbohydrates, breads made from white flour also provide a valuable source of soluble fibers which help lower cholesterol.

Homey White Bread

EVERY BREAD BAKER needs to have at least one good recipe for basic white bread with a thin, golden crust and a light crumb in their card file. This is mine, the sort of loaf you can set on the table with jars of peanut butter and grape jelly, and a quart of icy cold milk to wash it all down.

	REGULAR LOAF	LARGE LOAF
Water	½ cup	½ cup
Milk	⅔ cup	1 cup
Unsalted butter or vegetable oil	4 teaspoons	2 tablespoons
Salt	1¼ teaspoons	1½ teaspoons
Sugar	4 teaspoons	2 tablespoons
Bread flour	3 cups	4 cups
Dry yeast	2¼ teaspoons	2¼ teaspoons
	12 slices	*16 slices*

1. All ingredients must be at room temperature. Liquid ingredients should be approximately 80 degrees F. If using butter, cut into small cubes. Add ingredients in the order specified in your bread machine owner's manual.

2. Select white or basic bread and normal or medium crust.

3. Remove baked loaf from pan at the end of the baking cycle, and cool on a wire rack at least one hour before slicing.

Approximate Nutritional Analysis per Slice: 126 calories, 4 g protein, 23 g carbohydrates, 1 g fiber, 2 g fat, 1 mg cholesterol, 33 mg potassium, 185 mg sodium.

Baker's Note

For a homey look, lightly dust the top of the rising loaf with flour before it begins to bake.

Variations: Substitute honey for the sugar. For a regular loaf add 4 tea-spoons; for a large loaf add 2 tablespoons. The resulting bread will have a mellow flavor and a more golden crumb.

Sometimes, when I am in the mood for a basic loaf of bread with crunch and fiber, I'll add some wheat germ to this recipe. When making a regular loaf add ⅓ cup of wheat germ; ½ cup for a large loaf. For a sweeter loaf, use wheat germ flavored with honey.

Variation: Known for their excellent bread, French bakers will sometimes add small amounts of rye flour to their basic white-flour breads, as a way to enhance the texture and aroma of the crumb while, at the same time, strengthening the dough. When this technique is used in bread machines, the rye flour can help reduce the incidence of wrinkled tops. You may wish to try this technique if you have some rye flour handy. Add 2 tablespoons to any regular loaf recipe and 3 tablespoons to a large loaf.

Old-Fashioned Buttermilk White

ADDING BUTTERMILK TO FARMHOUSE LOAVES was an act of thriftiness on the part of the farm wife, using up the buttermilk that remained after churning butter. Perhaps not as popular as in years gone by, buttermilk gives bread a special tenderness and mellow flavor.

	REGULAR LOAF	LARGE LOAF
Water	⅓ cup	⅓ cup
Buttermilk	¾ cup	1 cup
Unsalted butter or vegetable oil	2 tablespoons	3 tablespoons
Salt	1½ teaspoons	1½ teaspoons
Dark brown sugar	4 teaspoons	2 tablespoons
Bread flour	3 cups	4 cups
Dry yeast	2¼ teaspoons	1 tablespoon
	12 slices	*16 slices*

1. All ingredients must be at room temperature. Liquid ingredients should be approximately 80 degrees F. If using butter, cut into small cubes. Add ingredients in the order specified in your bread machine owner's manual.

2. Select white or basic bread and normal or medium crust.

3. Remove baked loaf from pan at the end of the baking cycle, and cool on a wire rack at least one hour before slicing.

Approximate nutritional analysis per slice: 128 calories, 4 g protein, 22 g carbohydrates, 1 g fiber, 3 g fat, 6 mg cholesterol, 39 mg potassium, 284 mg sodium.

Variations: Substitute honey for the sugar. For a regular loaf add 4 teaspoons; for a large loaf add 2 tablespoons. The resulting bread will have a mellow flavor and a more golden crumb.

Baker's Note

After removing the bread from the pan, rub a tablespoon of cold butter over the top and sides of the hot loaf as it cools on the wire rack.

Real Farmhouse Potato Bread

EATEN BOILED, baked, fried, and mashed, the humble potato of the Incas has been called upon over the centuries to feed entire nations. In fact, when flour was in short supply on pioneer homesteads and piles of potatoes in the root cellar abundant, many were boiled and mashed to add to bread dough.

With a fluffy, soft crumb, this is a very distinctive loaf that holds up well for sandwiches or spread thick with homemade preserves.

	REGULAR LOAF	LARGE LOAF
Potato water (reserved)	½ cup	¾ cup
Milk	⅓ cup	½ cup
Unsalted butter or vegetable oil	4 teaspoons	2 tablespoons
Russet potato, large	1	1
Salt	1½ teaspoons	2 teaspoons
Sugar	4 teaspoons	2 tablespoons
Bread flour	3 cups	4 cups
Dry yeast	2¼ teaspoons	1 tablespoon
	12 slices	*16 slices*

1. Prepare mashed potato. Peel and cut a large russet potato into chunks. Place in a small saucepan and fill with just enough water to cover. Bring to a boil and cook until soft. Drain, reserve liquid; if necessary, add additional water until you have the amount specified in the recipe. Mash the potato until smooth, reserving ½ cup for a regular loaf and ¾ cup for a large loaf.

2. All ingredients must be at room temperature. Liquid ingredients should be approximately 80 degrees F. If using butter, cut into small cubes. Add ingredients in the order specified in your bread machine owner's manual.

continued on next page

Baker's Note

After removing the bread from the pan, rub a tablespoon of cold butter over the top and sides of the hot loaf as it cools on the wire rack.

Real Farmhouse Potato Bread (*cont.*)

3. Select white or basic bread and normal or medium crust.

4. Remove baked loaf from pan at the end of the baking cycle and cool on a wire rack at least one hour before slicing.

Approximate nutritional analysis per slice: 129 calories, 4 g protein, 20 g carbohydrates, 1 g fiber, 2 g fat, 1 mg cholesterol, 43 mg potassium, 5 mg sodium.

Variations: The addition of seeds like poppy or caraway add a nice country crunch to this bread. Add 1½ tablespoons of either to the regular loaf, or 2 tablespoons when making a large loaf.

Fresh-snipped or dried dill or chives also pair perfectly with this bread, with or without seeds. Add 2 tablespoons fresh-snipped dill or chives, or 2 teaspoons dried when making the regular loaf or 3 tablespoons fresh-snipped dill or 1 tablespoon dried for the large loaf recipe.

Chocolatey Walnut-Brownie Bread

RICH AND CHOCOLATEY, this bread draws crowds even before it's out of the machine. Like a good, chewy brownie, it's chock-full of walnuts. Great eaten alone or slathered with peanut butter, slices of this bread will be the hands-down winner during brown-bag trading sessions around the lunchroom table.

	REGULAR LOAF	LARGE LOAF
Water	⅓ cup	½ cup
Milk	⅔ cup	1 cup
Unsalted butter	5 tablespoons	7 tablespoons
Salt	1 teaspoon	1¼ teaspoons
Dark-brown sugar	⅓ cup packed	½ cup packed
Unsweetened cocoa	5 tablespoons	8 tablespoons
Bread flour	3 cups	4 cups
Dry yeast	2¼ teaspoons	1 tablespoon
Chopped walnuts, lightly toasted	⅔ cup	1 cup
	12 slices	*16 slices*

1. All ingredients must be at room temperature. Liquid ingredients should be approximately 80 degrees F. Cut butter into small cubes. Add ingredients in the order specified in your bread machine owner's manual. Walnuts can be added 5 minutes before the end of the last kneading cycle.

2. Select white or basic bread and light crust.

3. Remove baked loaf from pan at the end of the baking cycle, and cool on a wire rack at least one hour before slicing.

Approximate nutritional analysis per slice: 212 calories, 6 g protein, 28 g carbohydrates, 2 g fiber, 10 g fat, 14 mg cholesterol, 115 mg potassium, 188 mg sodium.

Baker's Note

So that the crust of this bread stays soft, rub a tablespoon of cold butter over the top and sides of the hot loaf, and cover with a clean cotton dishcloth as it cools.

Cinnamon-Raisin Bread

CINNAMON, ONCE USED TO PERFUME the wealthy citizens of Ancient Rome, is still cherished for its aromatic, spicy tones when used in baking such classics as cinnamon-raisin bread.

	REGULAR LOAF	LARGE LOAF
Water	⅓ cup	½ cup
Milk	½ cup	¾ cup
Egg, extra-large	1	1
Unsalted butter or vegetable oil	4 teaspoons	2 tablespoons
Vanilla extract	1 teaspoon	1½ teaspoons
Cinnamon	1 teaspoon	1½ teaspoons
Salt	1 teaspoon	1½ teaspoons
Dark-brown sugar	4 teaspoons	2 tablespoons
Bread flour	3 cups	4 cups
Dry yeast	2¼ teaspoons	2¼ teaspoons
Raisins	½ cup	¾ cup
	12 slices	*16 slices*

1. All ingredients must be at room temperature. Liquid ingredients should be approximately 80 degrees F. If using butter, cut into small cubes. Add ingredients in the order specified in your bread machine owner's manual. Raisins can be added 5 minutes before the end of the last kneading cycle.

2. Select white or basic bread and normal or medium crust.

3. Remove baked loaf from pan at the end of the baking cycle, and cool on a wire rack at least one hour before slicing.

Variations: Chopped, toasted walnuts add a nice twist to basic cinnamon-raisin bread. When making a regular loaf add ⅓ cup of walnuts along with the raisins; ½ cup for a large loaf.

Approximate nutritional analysis per slice: 158 calories, 5 g protein, 28 g carbohydrates, 1 g fiber, 3 g fat, 21 mg cholesterol, 33 mg potassium, 191 mg sodium.

Cornmeal Honey Loaf

MY FRIEND SHARON first introduced me to this bread. One of the signature loaves from Amy's Bakery in New York City, it's a somewhat dense bread sweetened with both golden and dark raisins, and the licorice flavor of fennel seed. For added crunch, this fantastic, delightful bread is made with coarsely ground golden cornmeal, which adds body and texture, making the sort of loaf that you absentmindedly nibble away at, until, before you know it, there's only a small sliver left.

After some trial and error, this is my version of this great bread made in the bread machine.

	REGULAR LOAF	LARGE LOAF
Water	½ cup	⅔ cup
Buttermilk	¾ cup	1 cup
Extra-virgin olive oil	2 tablespoons	3 tablespoons
Salt	1 teaspoon	1½ teaspoons
Honey	3 tablespoons	4 tablespoons
Fennel seeds	1 tablespoon	4 teaspoons
Yellow cornmeal, coarsely ground	½ cup	⅔ cup
Bread flour	3 cups	4 cups
Dry yeast	2¼ teaspoons	2¼ teaspoons
Golden raisins	2 tablespoons	3 tablespoons
Dark raisins or dried currants	2 tablespoons	3 tablespoons
	12 slices	*16 slices*

1. All ingredients must be at room temperature. Liquid ingredients should be approximately 80 degrees F. Add ingredients in the order specified in your bread machine owner's manual. Raisins can be added 5 minutes before the end of the last kneading cycle.

2. Select white or basic bread and normal or medium crust.

3. Remove baked loaf from pan at the end of the baking cycle, and cool on a wire rack at least one hour before slicing.

Approximate nutritional analysis per slice: 172 calories, 5 g protein, 32 g carbohydrates, 1 g fiber, 3 g fat, 1 mg cholesterol, 78 mg potassium, 199 mg sodium.

Irish Freckle Bread

ACCORDING TO THE IRISH, the dried black currants in this traditional bread look like freckles, hence the bread's name. The caraway seeds are optional, although I personally like the flavor that they add to the bread. For that special homemade look, sprinkle the baked loaf lightly with some flour.

	REGULAR LOAF	LARGE LOAF
Water	½ cup	½ cup
Buttermilk	¾ cup	1 cup
Unsalted butter	3 tablespoons	4 tablespoons
Salt	1¼ teaspoons	1½ teaspoons
Sugar	2 tablespoons	3 tablespoons
Caraway seeds	1 teaspoon	1½ teaspoons
Bread flour	3 cups	4 cups
Dry yeast	2¼ teaspoons	2¼ teaspoons
Dried black currants	½ cup	⅔ cup
	12 slices	*16 slices*

1. All ingredients must be at room temperature. Liquid ingredients should be approximately 80 degrees F. Cut butter into small cubes. Add ingredients in the order specified in your bread machine owner's manual. Currants can be added 5 minutes before the end of the last kneading cycle.

2. Select white or basic bread and normal or medium crust.

3. Remove baked loaf from pan at the end of the baking cycle, and cool on a wire rack at least one hour before slicing.

Approximate nutritional analysis per slice: 150 calories, 5 g protein, 26 g carbohydrates, 1 g fiber, 4 g fat, 8 mg cholesterol, 92 mg potassium, 240 mg sodium.

Old-Fashioned Oat Bread

OATS HAVE AN OLD-FASHIONED, natural goodness to them. Rich in minerals and protein, they are also known to aid in lowering cholesterol levels. When added as an ingredient to bread, they give the loaf a wholesome, nutty flavor and a chewy texture.

	REGULAR LOAF	LARGE LOAF
Water	½ cup	⅔ cup
Milk	¾ cup	1 cup
Unsalted butter	2 tablespoons	3 tablespoons
Salt	1½ teaspoons	2 teaspoons
Honey	3 tablespoons	4 tablespoons
Rolled oats	⅓ cup	½ cup
Bread flour	3 cups	4 cups
Dry yeast	2¼ teaspoons	2¼ teaspoons
	12 slices	*16 slices*

1. All ingredients must be at room temperature. Liquid ingredients should be approximately 80 degrees F. Cut butter into small cubes. Add ingredients in the order specified in your bread machine owner's manual.

2. Select white or basic bread and normal or medium crust.

3. Remove baked loaf from pan at the end of the baking cycle, and cool on a wire rack at least one hour before slicing.

Approximate nutritional analysis per slice: 150 calories, 5 g protein, 27 g carbohydrates, 1 g fiber, 3 g fat, 6 mg cholesterol, 45 mg potassium, 275 mg sodium.

continued on next page

Baker's Note

Gently brush top of rising loaf with vegetable oil and sprinkle lightly with some rolled oats, at least 10 minutes before the bread machine begins to bake.

Old-Fashioned Oat Bread (*cont.*)

Variations: Substitute real maple syrup for the honey. To make a regular loaf replace the honey with 3 tablespoons of real maple syrup. For a large loaf, replace the honey with 4 tablespoons of real maple syrup.

Add dried black currants or toasted, chopped walnuts, or a combination of the two, ½ cup for a regular loaf, and ¾ cup for a large loaf, 5 minutes before the end of the last kneading cycle.

Sourdough Starter

YEARS AGO, before the days of commercially manufactured yeast, yeast spores from the air were collected by Mother Nature and trapped in starchy water, where they would ferment and produce a bubbly starter. Nowadays, the easiest way to prepare homemade sourdough starter is to combine flour and organic milk with some plain yogurt, which contains active bacteria cultures, as used in the following, foolproof starter recipe.

1 cup nonfat or low-fat organic milk
3 tablespoons plain yogurt with active cultures (without any gelatin or thickening starches)
1 cup all-purpose, unbleached flour

Makes approximately 16 ounces starter

1. Pour boiling water into a 2-cup thermos to sterilize and warm.

2. Heat the milk in a small saucepan until lukewarm (90–100 degrees F). Remove from heat, and stir in the yogurt. Pour the hot water out of the thermos, and fill with the yogurt mixture. Cover tightly and let sit undisturbed 10 to 12 hours, or until thickened. Do not open or move mixture for at least 10 hours.

3. Pour thickened yogurt mixture into a small mixing bowl and stir in flour. Pour back into thermos, cover tightly, and let stand 2 to 5 days, or until the starter is full of bubbles and has acquired a pleasant sour smell.

4. To store, pour into a sterilized 1-quart glass jar and refrigerate. If a clear liquid forms on top, stir to blend. If liquid is pink, discard the starter.

5. Starter will keep up to a month in the refrigerator without feeding.

Note: If, at any time, the starter discolors or develops mold, discard starter and sterilize all containers before preparing new starter.

6. To replenish starter, combine 1 cup starter with 1 cup warm (90–100 degrees F) nonfat or low-fat milk and 1 cup unbleached, all-purpose flour. Pour into a sterilized 1-quart glass jar, cover tightly, and let sit in a warm place (80–90 degrees F) for 12 to 24 hours, or until bubbly and a clear liquid has formed on top. Stir before using and store in the refrigerator.

Sourdough White Bread

FOR WELL OVER TEN THOUSAND YEARS, man has been saving pieces of risen dough to use in making his next loaf of bread, known today as sourdough bread.

Traditionally, a good loaf of sourdough has a crisp crust, chewy crumb, and tangy distinct flavor, not unlike the great loaf you can make in your bread machine using the following recipe.

	REGULAR LOAF	LARGE LOAF
Water	⅔ cup	¾ cup
Sourdough starter, page 47	1 cup	1⅓ cup
Vegetable oil	2 tablespoons	3 tablespoons
Salt	1 teaspoon	2 teaspoons
Sugar	1 tablespoon	4 teaspoons
Rye flour	¼ cup	⅓ cup
Bread flour	3 cups	4 cups
Dry yeast	2¼ teaspoons	1 tablespoon
	12 slices	*16 slices*

1. All ingredients must be at room temperature. Liquid ingredients should be approximately 80 degrees F. Add ingredients in the order specified in your bread machine owner's manual.

2. Select white or basic bread and normal or medium crust.

3. Remove baked loaf from pan at the end of the baking cycle, and cool on a wire rack at least one hour before slicing.

Approximate nutritional analysis per slice: 156 calories, 5 g protein, 28 g carbohydrates, 1 g fiber, 4 g fat, 1 mg cholesterol, 46 mg potassium, 186 mg sodium.

Salt-Rising Bread Starter

SALT-RISING BREAD is an heirloom bread, from the days before central heating and commercially made yeast. In order to get bread to rise without having to maintain a sourdough-type starter, the family bread baker would prepare homemade yeast overnight, by mixing starchy ingredients like potatoes and cornmeal with hot water and sugar. If they were lucky, some yeast spores would settle in, the starter would take and be bubbly the next morning, ready for bread baking.

Since yeast spores need warmth to multiply and grow, the mixture had to be kept warm, not a small task in drafty, unheated houses. In order to do so, the starter was mixed and fermented in small stoneware crocks or glass jars packed in a pail of salt that had been warmed by the fire, acting as a thermal covering, therefore, leading to the name salt-rising bread.

The starter for this bread has to be prepared overnight, or at least ten to sixteen hours before you plan to make bread. The starter must be used within twenty-four hours and cannot be saved, so plan accordingly.

1 cup thinly sliced, peeled potatoes
1 tablespoon cornmeal
1 tablespoon sugar
¼ teaspoon baking soda
1 cup boiling water

Makes approximately 9 ounces starter

1. Combine all ingredients in a sterilized 1-quart glass jar. Cover, but not tightly, and place in a waterproof, self-locking plastic bag inside a small, six-pack-sized cooler. Fill the plastic bag with warm water (90 to 100 degrees F), so that it covers two-thirds of the jar. Cover or close the cooler and let the mixture set overnight, or at least 10 to 16 hours, undisturbed. When you open the cooler the next day, you should see a layer of foam on top of the liquid, and it should have a distinct sour smell to it.

2. Pour off the liquid into a clean container and save. Discard the solids. Proceed with recipe for salt-rising bread.

Salt-Rising Bread

SALT-RISING BREAD is an ideal sandwich loaf with a distinct pleasant smell and flavor and fine, golden crumb. Since the starter takes at least ten hours to prepare, plan accordingly.

For convenience, the starter is used primarily for flavoring, while commercially made, active dry yeast is used to assure a well-risen loaf.

	REGULAR LOAF	LARGE LOAF
Water	¾ cup	1 cup
Salt-rising starter, page 49	⅓ cup	½ cup
Vegetable oil	1 tablespoon	4 teaspoons
Salt	1 teaspoon	1¼ teaspoons
Instant nonfat dry milk	¼ cup	⅓ cup
Bread flour	3 cups	4 cups
Dry yeast	2¼ teaspoons	2¼ teaspoons
	12 slices	*16 slices*

1. All ingredients must be at room temperature. Liquid ingredients should be approximately 80 degrees F. Add ingredients in the order specified in your bread machine owner's manual.

2. Select basic cycle and normal or medium crust.

3. Remove baked loaf from pan at the end of the baking cycle, and cool on a wire rack at least one hour before slicing.

Approximate nutritional analysis per slice: 116 calories, 5 g protein, 21 g carbohydrates, 1 g fiber, 2 g fat, 0 mg cholesterol, 36 mg potassium, 186 mg sodium.

Basic Chinese Bun Dough

BELIEVE IT OR NOT, bread does have a place in Chinese cooking, especially steamed breads, like savory filled buns. Besides being delicious and highly addictive, Chinese steamed buns are quick and easy to prepare when using the bread machine to make the dough. To save even more time, the fillings are made from take-out dishes from your local Chinese takeout restaurant. Any leftover steamed buns can be frozen and then re-heated in the microwave oven.

1 cup water
1 tablespoon toasted sesame oil
2 tablespoons sugar
2 tablespoons finely chopped chives or scallion greens
3 cups bread flour
1 teaspoon baking powder
1½ teaspoons dry yeast

1. All ingredients must be at room temperature. Liquid ingredients should be approximately 80 degrees F. Add ingredients in the order specified in your bread machine owner's manual.

2. Select manual/dough.

3. At the end of the cycle let dough rest 5 minutes, then proceed with any recipes for Chinese steamed buns, pages 52 to 53.

Steamed Barbecued-Pork Buns

THESE BUNS ARE A CLASSIC. For added flavor, throw in any vegetables that may come with the pork take-out dish and chop up along with the meat. I would, however, eliminate any leafy greens or baby corn.

---

1 recipe Basic Chinese Bun Dough, page 51

---

1 order (approximately 1 pound) sliced Chinese boneless roast pork in barbecue or garlic sauce from your favorite Chinese takeout

---

Makes 16 steamed buns

1. Remove roast pork from sauce, reserving sauce, and chop pork into very small pieces in a food processor. Combine with ¼ cup reserved barbecue or garlic sauce.

2. Roll bun dough on a lightly floured surface into a long cylinder, 1½ inches in diameter. Cut into 16 pieces. With your fingers, flatten once piece of the dough at a time into a 3-inch round. The edges should be thinner with a puffy 1-inch center.

3. Place a heaping tablespoon of pork filling in center of dough, and gather edges together, pressing to seal. Twist gathered edges to prevent them from opening. Repeat with remaining dough and filling.

4. Place the buns, gathered side down, 1 inch apart, on bamboo or metal steamer trays lined with parchment paper. Cover with a clean cloth and let rise in a warm, draft-free place, 15 minutes.

5. To steam buns, place bamboo steamer trays over a pan or wok of boiling water, or place metal steamers into a large, covered pot of boiling water. Steam buns over high heat 15 to 20 minutes, or until puffed and springy to the touch. If you are steaming a few tiers at the same time, rotate steamer trays midway though. Transfer steamed buns to a platter, and serve right away.

Approximate nutritional analysis per bun: 145 calories, 11 g protein, 17 g carbohydrates, 1 g fiber, 4 g fat, 22 mg cholesterol, 108 mg potassium, 50 mg sodium.

Buddha's Delightful Veggie Buns

WHAT EASIER WAY to get kids to eat their veggies than to camouflage them in a soft, puffy bun? Most vegetables and pressed tofu work well in this recipe, although I would stay away from leafy greens and baby corn.

---

1 recipe Basic Chinese Bun Dough, page 51

1 order (approximately 1 pound) mixed Chinese vegetables in barbecue garlic sauce from your favorite Chinese takeout

---

Makes 16 steamed buns

1. Remove vegetables from sauce, reserving sauce, and chop vegetables into very small pieces in a food processor. Combine with ¼ cup of reserved barbecue or garlic sauce.

2. Roll bun dough on a lightly floured surface into a long cylinder, 1½ inches in diameter. Cut into 16 pieces. With your fingers, flatten one piece of the dough at a time into a 3-inch round. The edges should be thinner with a puffy 1-inch center.

3. Place a heaping tablespoon of vegetable filling in center of dough, and gather edges together, pressing to seal. Twist gathered edges to prevent them from opening. Repeat with remaining dough and filling.

4. Place buns gathered side down, 1 inch apart, on bamboo or metal steamer trays lined with parchment paper. Cover with a clean cloth and let rise in a warm, draft-free place, 15 minutes.

5. To steam buns, place bamboo steamer trays over a pan or wok of boiling water, or place metal steamers into a large, covered pot of boiling water. Steam buns over high heat 15 to 20 minutes, or until puffed and springy to the touch. If you are steaming a few tiers at a time, rotate steamer trays midway through. Transfer steamed buns to a platter and serve right away.

Approximate nutritional analysis per bun: 100 calories, 4 g protein, 20 g carbohydrates, 1 g fiber, 1 g fat, 0 mg cholesterol, 75 mg potassium, 192 mg sodium.

WHEN MAKING BREAD, EGGS CAN TURN SIMPLE, ORDINARY dough into something special. With a golden crumb and a richer, darker crust, these are memorable breads to be enjoyed at any time of day.

Egg breads can be savory with the addition of seeds, chopped onions or herbs, or sweet with fruit and spices, or covered with sugary glazes. They also come in infinite shapes and sizes, from a basic loaf to braided breads, as well as small rolls for breakfast or dinner.

Golden Egg Breads

Savory Egg Bread

AS THE FIRST BREAD IN THIS CHAPTER, the following recipe will serve as an introduction to using eggs in yeast bread baking. Besides adding rich yellow color to the crumb, the eggs impart a natural goodness to the flavor, as well as added height to the loaf. This is a perfect, all-purpose loaf equally good for toast or sandwiches, as well as with dinner.

	REGULAR LOAF	LARGE LOAF
Water	⅓ cup	⅓ cup
Milk	½ cup	½ cup
Egg, extra-large	1	2
Egg yolk, extra-large	1	1
Unsalted butter or vegetable oil	4 teaspoons	2 tablespoons
Salt	1 teaspoon	1½ teaspoons
Sugar	2 teaspoons	1 tablespoon
Bread flour	3 cups	4 cups
Dry yeast	2¼ teaspoons	2¼ teaspoons
	12 slices	*16 slices*

1. All ingredients must be at room temperature. Liquid ingredients should be approximately 80 degrees F. If using butter, cut into small cubes. Add ingredients in the order specified in your bread machine owner's manual. Do not use delay bake function.

2. Select white or basic bread and light crust.

3. Remove baked loaf from pan at the end of the baking program, and cool on a wire rack at least one hour before slicing.

continued on next page

Baker's Note

After removing the bread from the pan, rub a tablespoon of cold butter over the top and sides of the hot loaf as it cools.

Savory Egg Bread (*cont.*)

Approximate nutritional analysis per slice: 134 calories, 5 g protein, 22 g carbohydrates, 1 g fiber, 3 g fat, 39 mg cholesterol, 35 mg potassium, 190 mg sodium.

Variations: For added flavor and fiber, add ⅓ cup crunchy millet seeds, cracked wheat, or toasted sesame seeds (available in health-food or specialty-food stores) to a regular loaf and ½ cup to a large loaf.

Onion-Poppy-Seed Bread

THIS RECIPE IS A FAMILY FAVORITE, especially when used to make roasted chicken sandwiches with mayo and sliced tomato. The inspiration behind this bread is those soft, bakery-made egg rolls that are covered with chopped onion and poppy seeds. Since I could never get enough of either, I decided to add them directly to the dough, so that I could have some in each bite.

	REGULAR LOAF	LARGE LOAF
Water	1 cup	1 cup
Egg, extra large	1	2
Unsalted butter or vegetable oil	2 tablespoons	3 tablespoons
Salt	1½ teaspoons	2 teaspoons
Sugar	1 tablespoon	4 teaspoons
Dehydrated onions	¼ cup	⅓ cup
Poppy seeds	4 teaspoons	2 tablespoons
Bread flour	3 cups	4 cups
Dry yeast	2¼ teaspoons	2¼ teaspoons
	12 slices	*16 slices*

1. All ingredients must be at room temperature. Liquid ingredients should be approximately 80 degrees F. If using butter, cut into small cubes. Add ingredients in the order specified in your bread machine owner's manual. Do not use delay bake function.

2. Select white or basic bread and light crust.

3. Remove baked loaf from pan at the end of the baking program, and cool on a wire rack at least one hour before slicing.

Approximate nutritional analysis per slice: 137 calories, 5 g protein, 22 g carbohydrates, 1 g fiber, 4 g fat, 21 mg cholesterol, 25 mg potassium, 274 mg sodium.

Baker's Note

After removing the bread from the pan, rub a tablespoon of cold butter over the top and sides of the hot loaf as it cools.

Fresh Herb Bread

OVER THE YEARS I have come to enjoy the wide variety of herbs in my garden. It is amazing how a pinch of this and pinch of that can liven up a simple dish when cooking. The same happens when a combination of minced fresh herbs are added to rich egg dough. The resulting loaf is fragrant with the aroma and flavor of a summer garden.

	REGULAR LOAF	LARGE LOAF
Water	¾ cup	1 cup
Egg, extra-large	1	2
Olive oil	2 tablespoons	3 tablespoons
Honey	1 tablespoon	4 teaspoons
Salt	1½ teaspoons	2 teaspoons
Celery seed	1 teaspoon	1½ teaspoons
Combination of fresh, chopped herbs, such as: chives, parsley, basil, sage, dill, rosemary, thyme, or cilantro	¼ cup	⅓ cup
Bread flour	3 cups	4 cups
Dry yeast	2¼ teaspoons	2¼ teaspoons
	12 slices	*16 slices*

1. All ingredients must be at room temperature. Liquid ingredients should be approximately 80 degrees F. Add ingredients in the order specified in your bread machine owner's manual. Do not use delay bake function.

2. Select white or basic bread and light crust.

3. Remove baked loaf from pan at the end of the baking program, and cool on a wire rack at least one hour before slicing.

Approximate nutritional analysis per slice: 142 calories, 5 g protein, 23 g carbohydrates, 2 g fiber, 3 g fat, 21 mg cholesterol, 21 mg potassium, 186 mg sodium.

Sweet Bread

GLENNA, MY GOOD FRIEND AND COLLEAGUE, is also an excellent, experienced bread baker. While working on this book, she suggested that I try the following recipe. Being the doubting Thomas that I am, I wasn't sure that I wanted to include a bread made with a lemon-lime soft drink. Needless to say, I was surprised and impressed. The loaf is tender and sweet with a mild citrusy undertone, everything you look for in a good loaf of sweet bread.

By spicing up this loaf with colorful candied fruits and nuts, this recipe will soon become your best-kept secret during the holidays, when time is short and you need something festive to take to an office party or a get-together of family and friends.

	REGULAR LOAF	LARGE LOAF
7 UP	¾ cup	1 cup
Egg, extra-large	1	1
Egg yolk, extra-large	1	1
Unsalted butter	3 tablespoons	4 tablespoons
Salt	1½ teaspoons	2 teaspoons
Sugar	3 tablespoons	4 tablespoons
Bread flour	3 cups	4 cups
Dry yeast	2¼ teaspoons	2¼ teaspoons
	12 slices	*16 slices*

1. All ingredients must be at room temperature. Liquid ingredients should be approximately 80 degrees F. Cut butter into small cubes. Add ingredients in the order specified in your bread machine owner's manual. Do not use delay bake function.

2. Select sweet, white or basic bread and light crust.

3. Remove baked loaf from pan at the end of the baking program, and cool on a wire rack at least one hour before slicing.

Approximate nutritional analysis per slice: 146 calories, 5 g protein, 22 g carbohydrates, 1 g fiber, 4 g fat, 46 mg cholesterol, 21 mg potassium, 275 mg sodium.

continued on next page

Baker's Note

After removing the bread from the pan, rub a tablespoon of cold butter over the top and sides of the hot loaf as it cools.

Sweet Bread (*cont.*)

Variations: For a more intense citrusy flavor, add lemon or orange zest. Add 1 tablespoon to a regular loaf, or 4 teaspoons when making a large loaf.

The addition of ground, fragrant cardamom, toasted nuts like walnuts or pignoli, and candied cherries or citrus peel makes for an easy-to-prepare Christmas bread. Five minutes before the end of the last kneading program, add ¾ teaspoon cardamom, ½ cup candied fruit, and ¼ cup toasted nuts to a regular loaf, or 1 teaspoon of cardamom, ¾ cup of candied fruit and ⅓ cup nuts when making a large loaf. Sprinkle the baked loaf with confectioner's sugar after rubbing it with butter (see Baker's Note).

Orange-Cranberry-Walnut Loaf

ORANGES, CRANBERRIES, AND WALNUTS seem to be made for each other, especially when bound together in this colorful, sweet bread. Although one of my favorite breads to have on the sideboard Thanksgiving Day, I really enjoy it best the day after, with slices of leftover turkey and a dollop of cranberry relish.

	REGULAR LOAF	LARGE LOAF
Orange juice	⅓ cup	½ cup
Milk	⅓ cup	½ cup
Egg, extra-large	2	2
Unsalted butter	4 teaspoons	2 tablespoons
Grated orange zest	1 tablespoon	4 teaspoons
Salt	1 teaspoon	2 teaspoons
Sugar	1 tablespoon	4 teaspoons
Bread flour	3 cups	4 cups
Dry yeast	2¼ teaspoons	2¼ teaspoons
Dried cranberries	½ cup	⅔ cup
Toasted, chopped walnuts	⅓ cup	½ cup
	12 slices	*16 slices*

1. All ingredients must be at room temperature. Liquid ingredients should be approximately 80 degrees F. Cut butter into small cubes. Add ingredients in the order specified in your bread machine owner's manual. Do not use delay bake function. Cranberries and walnuts can be added 5 minutes before the end of the last kneading program.

2. Select white or basic bread and light crust.

3. Remove baked loaf from pan at the end of the baking program, and cool on a wire rack at least one hour before slicing.

Approximate nutritional analysis per slice: 160 calories, 6 g protein, 24 g carbohydrates, 1 g fiber, 5 g fat, 45 mg cholesterol, 67 mg potassium, 283 mg sodium.

Baker's Note

After removing the bread from the pan, rub a tablespoon of cold butter over the top and sides of the hot loaf as it cools.

Pumpkin-Pecan Bread

THIS IS THE FIRST OF A SERIES OF SWEETER, dessertlike breads made using the bread machine. While not as sweet as a loaf cake or quick bread, these breads are equally satisfying when the old sweet tooth becomes demanding. I especially enjoy the spicy taste of this bread.

	REGULAR LOAF	LARGE LOAF
Canned pumpkin	1 cup	1⅓ cup
Egg, extra-large	2	2
Unsalted butter	4 teaspoons	2 tablespoons
Vanilla extract	1½ teaspoons	2 teaspoons
Pumpkin-pie spice	1 tablespoon	4 teaspoons
Salt	1 teaspoon	1½ teaspoons
Brown sugar	3 tablespoons	4 tablespoons
Rolled oats	¼ cup	⅓ cup
Bread flour	3 cups	4 cups
Dry yeast	2¼ teaspoons	2¼ teaspoons
Raisins	⅓ cup	½ cup
Toasted, chopped pecans	½ cup	⅔ cup
	12 slices	*16 slices*

1. All ingredients must be at room temperature. Liquid ingredients should be approximately 80 degrees F. Cut butter into small cubes. Add ingredients in the order specified in your bread machine owner's manual. Do not use delay bake function. Raisins and pecans can be added 5 minutes before the end of the last kneading program.

2. Select sweet, white, or basic bread and light crust.

3. Remove baked loaf from pan at the end of the baking program and cool on a wire rack at least one hour before slicing.

Approximate nutritional analysis per slice: 192 calories, 6 g protein, 29 g carbohydrates, 2 g fiber, 6 g fat, 45 mg cholesterol, 131 mg potassium, 193 mg sodium.

Baker's Note

After removing the bread from the pan, rub a tablespoon of cold butter over the top and sides of the hot loaf as it cools.

Glazed Lemon Poppy-Seed Loaf

ONE OF MY FAVORITE bundt cakes is lemon poppy-seed with a tart lemon glaze. It reminds me of hot summer afternoons sitting in the shade with a frosty glass of iced tea and a buttery slice of this lemony cake. As a personal challenge, I wanted to see if I could come up with a yeast bread equal in taste to this highly caloric cake. Based on how quickly this bread disappears every time I make it, I think I've succeeded, but I'll let you be the judge of this blue-ribbon winner!

	REGULAR LOAF	LARGE LOAF
Water	1/3 cup	1/2 cup
Milk	1/2 cup	1/2 cup
Egg, extra-large	1	2
Unsalted butter	4 teaspoons	2 tablespoons
Salt	1 1/2 teaspoons	2 teaspoons
Sugar	2 tablespoons	3 tablespoons
Grated lemon zest	2 tablespoons	3 tablespoons
Poppy seeds	4 teaspoons	2 tablespoons
Bread flour	3 cups	4 cups
Dry yeast	2 1/4 teaspoons	2 1/4 teaspoons
	12 slices	*16 slices*

1. All ingredients must be at room temperature. Liquid ingredients should be approximately 80 degrees F. Cut butter into small cubes. Add ingredients in the order specified in your bread machine owner's manual. Do not use delay bake function.

2. Select sweet, white, or basic bread and light crust.

3. Remove baked loaf from pan at the end of the baking program and cool on a wire rack at least one hour before drizzling with glaze.

continued on next page

Glazed Lemon Poppy-Seed Loaf (*cont.*)

Lemon Glaze

2 teaspoons unsalted butter, softened
2 teaspoons grated lemon zest
4 tablespoons confectioners' sugar
2 teaspoons lemon juice

Cream butter with lemon zest and confectioners' sugar in a small bowl. Mix in the lemon juice until smooth. Drizzle glaze over cooled loaf of bread. Let dry before slicing.

Approximate nutritional analysis per slice: 137 calories, 5 g protein, 23 g carbohydrates, 1 g fiber, 3 g fat, 26 mg cholesterol, 32 mg potassium, 277 mg sodium.

Sweet Almond-and-Cherry Bread

ALMONDS AND CHERRIES are another fantastic flavor combination. The dried red cherries plump up fat and contrast nicely to the toasted almond slivers. This is a good bread to serve at breakfast or coffee time.

	REGULAR LOAF	LARGE LOAF
Water	⅓ cup	½ cup
Milk	⅓ cup	½ cup
Egg, extra-large	2	2
Unsalted butter	4 teaspoons	2 tablespoons
Almond extract	1½ teaspoons	2 teaspoons
Salt	1 teaspoon	1½ teaspoons
Sugar	2 tablespoons	3 tablespoons
Bread flour	3 cups	4 cups
Dry yeast	2¼ teaspoons	2¼ teaspoons
Dried cherries	½ cup	⅔ cup
Toasted, slivered almonds	½ cup	⅔ cup
	12 slices	*16 slices*

1. All ingredients must be at room temperature. Liquid ingredients should be approximately 80 degrees F. Cut butter into small cubes. Add ingredients in the order specified in your bread machine owner's manual. Do not use delay bake function. Cherries and almonds can be added 5 minutes before the end of the last kneading program.

2. Select sweet, white, or basic bread and light crust.

3. Remove baked loaf from pan at the end of the baking program and cool on a wire rack at least one hour before slicing.

Approximate nutritional analysis per slice: 202 calories, 7 g protein, 35 g carbohydrates, 2 g fiber, 6 g fat, 45 mg cholesterol, 75 mg potassium, 195 mg sodium.

Baker's Note

After removing the bread from the pan, rub a tablespoon of cold butter over the top and sides of the hot loaf as it cools. Sprinkle with confectioners' sugar if desired.

Challah

CHALLAH, A TRADITIONAL JEWISH EGG BREAD, is served in most Jewish homes for Sabbath meals and during festivals and holidays. This puffy, braided loaf is delicious served alone, or sliced thick and turned into French toast, served with fresh berries and real maple syrup.

½ cup water
2 extra-large eggs
1 extra-large egg yolk
3 tablespoons vegetable oil
1 tablespoon sugar
1 teaspoon salt
3 cups bread flour
2¼ teaspoons dry yeast
1 extra-large egg, beaten with 1 teaspoon water (egg wash)

12 slices

1. All ingredients must be at room temperature. Liquid ingredients should be approximately 80 degrees F. Add ingredients in the order specified in your bread machine owner's manual. Do not use delay bake function.

2. Select manual/dough.

3. At the end of the program, punch down the dough with your knuckles. Let dough rest 5 minutes.

Variations: Add ½ cup golden raisins to the bread machine 5 minutes before the end of the last kneading.

Sprinkle challah with poppy seeds after brushing with egg wash.

4. Lightly sprinkle work surface with flour. Divide dough into three equal pieces. Dampen hands and roll each piece into a 16-inch-long rope. Sprinkle dough with flour if too sticky. Lay ropes next to one another and pinch top ends together and tuck under. Braid ropes, pinch remaining ends together, and tuck under. Place on a lightly greased, large baking pan. Cover and let rise until doubled in bulk, about 1 to 1½ hours.

5. Preheat oven to 375 degrees F. Brush braid with egg wash, and bake 20 to 30 minutes, or until golden. Remove from oven and cool on wire rack.

Approximate nutritional analysis per slice: 162 calories, 6 g protein, 22 g carbohydrates, 1 g fiber, 6 g fat, 80 mg cholesterol, 31 mg potassium, 198 mg sodium.

Basic Dinner-Roll Dough

WHAT COULD BE BETTER than a basket of homemade dinner rolls hot and steaming from the oven, especially when the dough is made in a bread machine, requiring minimum attention and only a few minutes for hand shaping?

The following basic egg-dough recipe can be shaped in a variety of ways. I've given a couple of my favorites, as well as a variation for flaky, cheesy buns made with fresh-minced herbs.

¾ cup water
2 extra-large eggs
3 tablespoons unsalted butter
3 tablespoons sugar
1 teaspoon salt
3½ cups bread flour
2¼ teaspoons dry yeast

1. All ingredients must be at room temperature. Liquid ingredients should be approximately 80 degrees F. Cut butter into small pieces. Add ingredients in the order specified in your bread machine owner's manual. Do not use delay bake function.

2. Select manual/dough.

3. At the end of the program, punch down dough. Let dough rest 5 minutes.

4. Proceed with any of the recipes for shaping and baking, pages 69 to 75.

Parker House Rolls

THESE LIGHT, PUFFY ROLLS first became famous during the late nineteenth century, when they were served at the Parker House, a hotel in Boston.

1 recipe Basic Dinner-Roll Dough, page 68
1 extra-large egg, beaten with 1 teaspoon water (egg wash)

Makes 16 Rolls

1. Lightly grease a large baking pan. Lightly sprinkle work surface with flour. Roll dough into a 12-inch square. Trim to make edges straight. Cut into four equal sections, horizontally and vertically, so that you have sixteen, 3-inch squares of dough.

2. Slightly stretch each piece of dough to elongate it, then fold in half, a little off center. Place 1 inch apart on baking sheet.

3. Cover and let rise in a warm, draft-free location, until doubled in bulk, approximately 45 minutes to 1 hour.

continued on next page

Parker House Rolls (*cont.*)

4. Preheat oven to 350 degrees F. Brush with egg wash, and bake 15 to 18 minutes, or until golden brown.

Approximate nutritional analysis per roll: 12 calories, 4 g protein, 20 g carbohydrates, 1 g fiber, 3 g fat, 37 mg cholesterol, 18 mg potassium, 144 mg sodium.

Fan-Shaped Rolls

THESE ROLLS FAN OPEN as they rise and bake, making for a buttery, flaky dinner roll.

1 recipe Basic Dinner-Roll Dough, page 68
1 extra-large egg beaten with 1 teaspoon water (egg wash)

Makes 12 rolls

1. Lightly grease a 12-cup muffin pan. Lightly sprinkle work surface with flour. Roll dough into 18 x 8-inch rectangle. Trim to make edges straight.

continued on next page

Fan-Shaped Rolls (*cont.*)

2. Cut lengthwise into 1½-inch wide strips. Stack strips and cut into 1½-inch pieces. Place pieces, cut side up, in the muffin cups.

3. Cover and let rise in a warm, draft-free location, until doubled in bulk, approximately 45 minutes to 1 hour.

4. Preheat oven to 350 degrees F. Brush with egg wash and bake 15 to 18 minutes or until golden brown.

Approximate nutritional analysis per roll: 176 calories, 6 g protein, 27 g carbohydrates, 1 g fiber, 5 g fat, 67 mg cholesterol, 30 mg potassium, 197 mg sodium.

Cloverleaf Rolls

CLOVERLEAF ROLLS HAVE A RETRO 1950s look to them, and are easy and fun for children to help make and shape.

1 recipe Basic Dinner-Roll Dough, page 68
1 extra-large egg beaten with 1 teaspoon water (egg wash)
2 tablespoons poppy seeds

Makes 12 rolls

1. Lightly grease a 12-cup muffin pan. Divide dough in half, and each half into 6 equal parts. Tear each part into three pieces and shape into smooth balls. Place three balls in each muffin cup.

continued on next page

Cloverleaf Rolls (*cont.*)

2. Cover and let rise in a warm, draft-free location, until doubled in bulk, approximately 45 minutes to 1 hour.

3. Preheat oven to 350 degrees F. Brush with egg wash and sprinkle with poppy seeds.

4. Bake 15 to 18 minutes, or until golden brown.

Approximate nutritional analysis per roll: 177 calories, 6 g protein, 23 g carbohydrates, 1 g fiber, 5 g fat, 49 mg cholesterol, 35 mg potassium, 192 mg sodium.

Herb-and-Cheese Rolls

THE MELLOW FLAVOR of cheese paired with garden-fresh herbs makes these rolls very special indeed.

1 recipe Basic Dinner-Roll Dough, page 68
2 cups (8 ounces) shredded sharp Cheddar cheese
¼ cup snipped chives
3 tablespoons minced fresh herbs, such as oregano, thyme, marjoram, sage, or a combination
1 extra-large egg beaten with 1 teaspoon water (egg wash)

Makes 12 rolls

1. Follow recipe for dinner rolls, page 68. Add cheese, chives, and herbs, 5 minutes before the end of the last kneading program.

2. At the end of the program, punch down dough. Let dough rest 5 minutes.

3. Lightly grease a large 13-x-9-x-2-inch baking pan. Lightly flour dough and press to fit in pan evenly. Cover and let rise 45 minutes to 1 hour, or until doubled in bulk.

4. Using a dough scraper or kitchen knife, cut dough lengthwise into three even strips. Cut in the opposite direction 4 times to form 12 rolls.

5. Cover and let rise in a warm, draft-free location, until doubled in bulk, approximately 45 minutes to an hour.

6. Preheat oven to 350 degrees F. Brush with egg wash, and bake 15 to 18 minutes, or until golden brown.

Approximate nutritional analysis per roll: 247 calories, 11g protein, 28 g carbohydrates, 1 g fiber, 11 g fat, 69 mg cholesterol, 50 mg potassium, 309 mg sodium.

Suizos

I LIVED FOR TWO YEARS as an exchange student in Seville, Spain, when I was in my early twenties. Every morning I would trek to the closest cafe for my morning ritual of *café con leche* and either a *tostada con aceite*—grilled bread with olive oil—or, on those mornings when something sweet was in order, a *suizo*, a delicious sweet roll.

These wonderful breakfast rolls rise until puffy, at which time they are slashed on top and the opening filled with granulated sugar. After more years than I wish to remember, *suizos* still remain a personal favorite for breakfast or later in the day with a cup of coffee. Kids also like these, since they can lick the sugar off before getting to the roll.

1 cup water
2 extra-large eggs
3 tablespoons vegetable oil
½ cup sugar plus ¼ cup for topping
½ teaspoon salt
4 cups bread flour
2¼ teaspoons dry yeast
1 extra-large egg, beaten with 1 teaspoon water (egg wash)

Makes 12 rolls

1. All ingredients must be at room temperature. Liquid ingredients should be approximately 80 degrees F. Add ingredients in the order specified in your bread machine owner's manual. Do not use delay bake function.

2. Select manual/dough.

3. At the end of the program, punch down dough. Let dough rest 5 minutes.

4. Lightly grease two large baking pans. Lightly sprinkle work surface with flour. Divide dough in half, and each half into 6 equal pieces. Shape each piece into a smooth ball; shape each into a 4-

inch-long oval by gently rolling between the palms of your hands. Place rolls on prepared baking pans.

5. Cover and let rise in a warm, draft-free location, until doubled in bulk, approximately 1 to 1½ hours.

6. Preheat oven to 375 degrees F. Slash the rolls lengthwise down the center with a sharp knife or razor. Fill the slashes with 1 teaspoon of sugar. Brush the rolls with the beaten egg wash, taking care not to touch the sugar. Bake 10 to 15 minutes, or until golden brown. Remove from pans and cool on a wire rack.

Approximate nutritional analysis per roll: 233 calories, 7 g protein, 40 g carbohydrates, 1 g fiber, 5 g fat, 62 mg cholesterol, 30 mg potassium, 109 mg sodium.

Pandoro

ORIGINATING IN VERONA, ITALY, the hometown of the world's most famous star-crossed lovers, Romeo and Juliet, *pandoro* means "golden bread."

This Christmas yeast bread is traditionally baked in a tall, star-shaped pan, available at some specialty housewares retailers or by mail order from King Arthur Flour (1-800-827-6836). Almost cakelike, with a buttery crumb, *pandoro* is generously sprinkled with confectioners' sugar before serving. I specially like to slice the *pandoro* horizontally and arrange the slices slightly askew, one on top of the other, making it look like a snow-covered Christmas tree.

¾ cup water
2 extra-large eggs
5 tablespoons unsalted butter
2 teaspoons vanilla extract
2 teaspoons grated lemon zest
1½ teaspoons salt
⅓ cup sugar
4 cups all-purpose flour
2¼ teaspoons dry yeast
¼ cup golden raisins
¼ cup slivered almonds (optional)
3 tablespoons unsalted butter, melted
Confectioners' sugar, for dusting

16 slices

1. All ingredients must be at room temperature. Liquid ingredients should be approximately 80 degrees F. Cut butter into small cubes. Add ingredients in the order specified in your bread machine owner's manual. Do not use delay bake function. Raisins and slivered almonds can be added 5 minutes before the end of the last kneading program.

2. Select manual/dough.

3. At the end of the program, punch down dough. Let dough rest 5 minutes.

4. Place dough in a well-greased, star-shaped *pandoro* or angel-food-cake pan. Cover with plastic wrap and let rise until the dough has risen almost to the top of the pan (1½ to 1¾ hours).

5. Preheat oven to 350 degrees F. Bake 30 to 35 minutes, or until *pandoro* is golden brown, and an instant-read thermometer registers 190 degrees.

6. Let cool in pan 5 minutes on a wire rack. Carefully remove from pan, and brush *pandoro* with melted butter while still hot. Cool to room temperature and dust with confectioners' sugar before serving.

Approximate nutritional analysis per slice: 218 calories, 5 g protein, 32 g carbohydrates, 2 g fiber, 8 g fat, 47 mg cholesterol, 86 mg potassium, 212 mg sodium.

Basic Pull-Apart Bubble Bread Sweet Dough

PULL-APART YEAST BREAD, also known as bubble bread, first began to appear in women's magazines back in the 1950s, and it is a favorite with many baby boomers. Its different names refer to the method used to make and to serve the bread. A ball of risen, punch-down yeast dough is pulled apart into small pieces, rolled into balls or "bubbles," and placed in a 10-inch tube pan or angel-food-cake pan with other tasty things like sugar and melted butter. The baked sweet bread is then either cut into slices or pulled apart.

I like this bread so much that I have come up with three varieties that I am pleased to share with you.

1 cup milk
1 extra-large egg
2 tablespoons unsalted butter
1 teaspoon vanilla extract
½ teaspoon salt
4 tablespoons sugar
3½ cups bread flour
2¼ teaspoons dry yeast

1. All ingredients must be at room temperature. Liquid ingredients should be approximately 80 degrees F. Cut butter into small cubes. Add ingredients in the order specified in your bread machine owner's manual. Do not use delay bake function.

2. Select manual/dough.

3. At the end of the program, punch down dough. Let dough rest 5 minutes

4. Proceed with any recipe for pull-apart bread, pages 81 to 83.

Funny as a Monkey Chocolate-Crumb Pull-Apart Bread

THIS IS THE BREAD for all you chocolate lovers. Each piece, or bubble, of bread is covered with sugary chocolate crumbs.

---

1 recipe Basic Pull-Apart Bubble Bread Sweet Dough, page 80

---

1 cup finely crushed chocolate-cookie crumbs

¼ cup sugar

½ teaspoon ground cinnamon

---

4 tablespoons unsalted butter, melted

Makes 16 servings

1. Grease and flour a 10-inch tube pan or angel-food-cake pan.

2. Combine cookie crumbs, sugar, and cinnamon in a large bowl. Remove punched-down dough from bread machine, and divide into 32 equal pieces. Add dough and melted butter to the cookie crumb mixture and toss to coat.

3. Evenly layer covered dough pieces in prepared pan and let rise, uncovered, in a warm, draft-free place, until doubled in bulk, approximately 45 minutes to 1 hour.

4. Preheat oven to 350 degrees F. Bake 45 to 50 minutes, or until golden brown. Cool in the pan on a wire rack, 10 minutes. Remove from the pan, and cool completely on the rack before serving.

Approximate nutritional analysis per serving: 225 calories, 5 g protein, 36 g carbohydrates, 1 g fiber, 7 g fat, 27 mg cholesterol, 73 mg potassium, 181 mg sodium.

Apple-Chunk and Walnut Pull-Apart Bread

MOST DEFINITELY a homey-smelling and -tasting bread, fragrant with sweet apples and spices.

1 recipe Basic Pull-Apart Bubble Bread Sweet Dough, page 80
2 large Golden Delicious or Gala apples
2 teaspoons lemon juice
¼ cup sugar
½ teaspoon ground cinnamon
¼ teaspoon ground nutmeg
⅛ teaspoon ground cloves
¼ cup finely chopped walnuts
3 tablespoons unsalted butter, melted

Makes 16 servings

1. Grease and flour a 10-inch tube pan or angel-food-cake pan. Peel and core apples. Cut into small dice. Toss with lemon juice in a large mixing bowl. Combine sugar, cinnamon, nutmeg, cloves, and walnuts in a small bowl.

2. Remove punched-down dough from bread machine, and divide into 32 equal pieces. Add dough, sugar mixture, and melted butter to the apple mixture. Toss to coat.

3. Evenly layer dough-and-apple mixture in the prepared pan and let rise, uncovered, in a warm, draft-free location, until doubled in bulk, approximately 45 minutes to an hour.

4. Preheat oven to 350 degrees F. Bake 45 to 50 minutes, or until golden brown. Cool in the pan on a wire rack, 10 minutes. Remove from the pan, and cool completely on the rack before serving.

Approximate nutritional analysis per serving: 179 calories, 5 g protein, 28 g carbohydrates, 1 g fiber, 6 g fat, 24 mg cholesterol, 70 mg potassium, 80 mg sodium.

Tropical Hawaiian Bubble Bread

CRUSHED PINEAPPLE AND COCONUT add moistness to this tropical variation; the nuts add some crunch.

1 recipe Basic Pull-Apart Bubble Bread Sweet Dough, page 80
16-ounce can crushed pineapple
½ cup shredded sweetened coconut
¼ cup finely chopped pecans or macadamia nuts
¼ cup brown sugar
3 tablespoons unsalted butter, melted

Makes 16 servings

1. Grease and flour a 10-inch tube pan or angel-food-cake pan. Drain pineapple, reserving 2 tablespoons juice. Combine pineapple, reserved juice, and coconut in a large mixing bowl.

2. Remove punched-down dough from bread machine and divide into 32 equal pieces. Add the dough, pecans, brown sugar, and melted butter to the pineapple mixture and toss to coat.

3. Evenly layer the dough and pineapple mixture in the prepared pan and let rise, uncovered, in a warm, draft-free location, until doubled in bulk, approximately 45 minutes to 1 hour.

4. Preheat oven to 350 degrees F. Bake 45 to 50 minutes, or until golden brown. Cool in the pan on a wire rack, 10 minutes. Remove from the pan, and cool completely on the rack before serving.

Approximate nutritional analysis per serving: 195 calories, 5 g protein, 30 g carbohydrates, 1 g fiber, 7 g fat, 24 mg cholesterol, 94 mg potassium, 88 mg sodium.

MILLED FROM THE ENTIRE WHEAT KERNEL, WHOLE-WHEAT flour adds flavor, texture, and fiber to bread and baked goods. When added to white-bread flour, the resulting loaves have greater body, while still retaining a light texture. These make for wonderful breads especially when combined with other grains, fruits, seeds, and nuts, as well as fragrant spices.

Breads made with 100 percent whole-wheat flour are denser, with more of an earthy flavor. Fortunately, newer model

Whole-Grain Goodness

bread machines can usually handle these heavier doughs effortlessly, with excellent results.

Golden Wheat Bread

THIS RECIPE PROVIDES the perfect balance between white and whole-wheat flour making for a loaf that rises high and is the color of golden sheaves of wheat. This is a basic recipe that can be changed and adapted by adding other ingredients, like raisins and cinnamon or crunchy seeds.

	REGULAR LOAF	LARGE LOAF
Water	¼ cup	⅓ cup
Milk	½ cup	⅔ cup
Egg, extra-large	1	1
Unsalted butter	2 tablespoons	3 tablespoons
Salt	1½ teaspoons	2 teaspoons
Honey	3 tablespoons	4 tablespoons
Bread flour	2¼ cups	2⅔ cups
Whole-wheat flour	¾ cup	1⅓ cups
Dry yeast	2¼ teaspoons	2¼ teaspoons
	12 slices	*16 slices*

1. All ingredients must be at room temperature. Liquid ingredients should be approximately 80 degrees F. Cut butter into small cubes. Add ingredients in the order specified in your bread machine owner's manual. Do not use delay bake function.

2. Select basic or whole-wheat bread, and normal or medium crust.

3. Remove baked loaf from pan at the end of the baking cycle, and cool on a wire rack at least one hour before slicing.

Approximate nutritional analysis per slice: 146 calories, 5 g protein, 25 g carbohydrates, 2 g fiber, 3 g fat, 27 mg cholesterol, 37 mg potassium, 279 mg sodium.

continued on next page

Baker's Note

After removing the bread from the pan, rub a tablespoon of cold butter over the top and sides of the hot loaf as it cools.

Golden Wheat Bread (*cont.*)

Variations: The addition of raisins and cinnamon to this bread makes a delicious whole-wheat raisin-cinnamon loaf. Five minutes before the end of the last kneading cycle, add 1 teaspoon ground cinnamon and ½ cup raisins to a regular loaf and 1½ teaspoons ground cinnamon and ⅔ cup raisins when making a large loaf.

The addition of seeds like poppy, sesame, flax, and millet add a nice crunch to this bread. Add 1½ tablespoons of your favorite seeds to the regular loaf or 2 tablespoons when making a large loaf.

Wheat-Flake Potato Bread

THIS BREAD IS SO GOOD FOR YOU, it even looks healthy. But, best of all, it tastes great. High in fiber and complex carbohydrates, it has a nice, tender crumb thanks to the potato, and a slight chew from the wheat flakes (available at your local health-food store). This is a good, all-purpose bread.

	REGULAR LOAF	LARGE LOAF
Potato water (reserved)	1 cup	1¼ cups
Vegetable oil	2 tablespoons	3 tablespoons
Russet potato, large	1	1
Salt	1½ teaspoons	2 teaspoons
Sugar	4 teaspoons	2 tablespoons
Wheat flakes	⅔ cup	1 cup
Bread flour	1½ cups	2 cups
Whole-wheat flour	1½ cups	2 cups
Dry yeast	2¼ teaspoons	2¼ teaspoons
	12 slices	*16 slices*

1. Prepare mashed potato. Peel and cut a large russet potato into chunks. Place in a small saucepan and cover with three cups of water. Bring to a boil and cook until soft. Drain, reserve liquid. Mash the potato, reserving ½ cup for a regular loaf and ⅔ cup for a large loaf.

2. Pour hot potato water over the wheat flakes in a small bowl. Let soak 10 minutes. Drain wheat flakes and reserve the liquid. If necessary, add additional water until you have the amount specified.

3. All ingredients must be at room temperature. Liquid ingredients should be approximately 80 degrees F. Add ingredients in the order specified in your bread machine owner's manual. Reserve two tablespoons of soaked wheat flakes for the top of the loaf.

continued on next page

Wheat-Flake Potato Bread (*cont.*)

4. Select whole-wheat or basic bread and normal or medium crust.

5. Approximately 10 minutes before the bread machine begins to bake, gently brush top of rising loaf with vegetable oil and sprinkle with the reserved wheat flakes.

6. Remove baked loaf from pan at the end of the baking cycle and cool on a wire rack at least one hour before slicing.

Approximate nutritional analysis per slice: 138 calories, 5 g protein, 24 g carbohydrates, 3 g fiber, 3 g fat, 0 mg cholesterol, 67 mg potassium, 179 mg sodium.

Banana-Raisin Oat Bread

YOU DON'T OFTEN FIND yeast-bread recipes that call for bananas. While the initial recipe was chewy with oats, with a perfect balance of sweetness from the honey and raisins, it seemed to be missing something in the flavor. After having eaten a slice for breakfast, I began to snack on a banana which turned out to be the missing link needed to turn a good bread into a great one. I especially enjoy this bread toasted, spread with chunky peanut butter and grape jelly.

	REGULAR LOAF	LARGE LOAF
Milk	½ cup	⅔ cup
Egg, extra-large	1	1
Unsalted butter	2 tablespoons	3 tablespoons
Mashed ripe banana	½ cup	⅔ cup
Salt	1½ teaspoons	2 teaspoons
Honey	2 tablespoons	3 tablespoons
Rolled oats	¼ cup	⅓ cup
Bread flour	2¼ cups	3 cups
Whole-wheat flour	¾ cup	1 cup
Dry yeast	2¼ teaspoons	2¼ teaspoons
Raisins	2 tablespoons	3 tablespoons
Golden raisins	2 tablespoons	3 tablespoons
	12 slices	*16 slices*

Baker's Note

Approximately 10 minutes before the bread machine begins to bake, gently brush the top of the rising loaf with vegetable oil and sprinkle lightly with some rolled oats.

1. All ingredients must be at room temperature. Liquid ingredients should be approximately 80 degrees F. Cut butter into small cubes. Add ingredients in the order specified in your bread machine owner's manual.

2. Select whole-wheat or basic bread and normal or medium crust.

continued on next page

Banana-Raisin Oat Bread (*cont.*)

3. Remove baked loaf from pan at the end of the baking cycle and cool on a wire rack at least one hour before slicing.

Approximate nutritional analysis per slice: 162 calories, 5 g protein, 29 g carbohydrates, 2 g fiber, 3 g fat, 27 mg cholesterol, 101 mg potassium, 279 mg sodium.

Variations: Add toasted chopped walnuts, ½ cup for a regular loaf, and ⅔ cup for a large loaf, 5 minutes before the end of the last kneading cycle.

PBJ (Peanut-Butter-and-Jelly) Bread

I HAVE YET TO SEE A KID, and rarely adults, turn down a PBJ sandwich so, I thought, why not give the sandwich a head start and add some peanut butter and chewy fruits, like dried cherries or blueberries, to a basic bread dough, making the most peanut buttery PBJ sandwich yet!

	REGULAR LOAF	LARGE LOAF
Water	½ cup	¾ cup
Milk	¼ cup	½ cup
Creamy peanut butter	⅓ cup	½ cup
Egg	1 extra-large	1 extra-large
Salt	1 teaspoon	1½ teaspoons
Honey	2 tablespoons	3 tablespoons
Bread flour	2 cups	2⅔ cups
Whole-wheat flour	1 cup	1⅓ cups
Dry yeast	2¼ teaspoons	2¼ teaspoons
Dried fruit, such as: cranberries, cherries, or blueberries	½ cup	⅔ cup
	12 slices	*16 slices*

1. All ingredients must be at room temperature. Liquid ingredients should be approximately 80 degrees F. Add ingredients in the order specified in your bread machine owner's manual. Dried fruit can be added 5 minutes before the end of the last kneading cycle.

2. Select white or basic bread and normal or medium crust.

3. Remove baked loaf from pan at the end of the baking cycle, and cool on a wire rack at least one hour before slicing.

Approximate nutritional analysis per slice: 194 calories, 7 g protein, 36 g carbohydrates, 3 g fiber, 5 g fat, 21 mg cholesterol, 78 mg potassium, 221 mg sodium

Multigrain Bread

EVERY GOOD BREAD BAKER has their own favorite multigrain bread recipe. This is one that I particularly like. It has the right balance of different grains, making a nutritious loaf that is not too heavy, with the added goodness of coarsely ground cornmeal and flax seeds for flavor and texture.

	REGULAR LOAF	LARGE LOAF
Water	1 cup	1¼ cups
Egg, extra-large	1	1
Vegetable oil	2 tablespoons	3 tablespoons
Salt	1½ teaspoons	2 teaspoons
Honey	3 tablespoons	4 tablespoons
Flax seeds	¼ cup	⅓ cup
Yellow cornmeal, coarsely ground	2 tablespoons	3 tablespoons
Rolled oats	2 tablespoons	3 tablespoons
Bread flour	2¼ cups	3 cups
Whole-wheat flour	¾ cup	1 cup
Rye flour	2 tablespoons	3 tablespoons
Dry yeast	2¼ teaspoons	2¼ teaspoons
	12 slices	*16 slices*

1. All ingredients must be at room temperature. Liquid ingredients should be approximately 80 degrees F. Add ingredients in the order specified in your bread machine owner's manual.

2. Select basic cycle and normal or medium crust.

3. Remove baked loaf from pan at the end of the baking cycle, and cool on a wire rack at least one hour before slicing.

Approximate nutritional analysis per slice: 154 calories, 5 g protein, 27 g carbohydrates, 2 g fiber, 3 g fat, 21 mg cholesterol, 29 mg potassium, 274 mg sodium.

100 Percent Whole-Wheat Bread

EVEN THOUGH I PERSONALLY PREFER some white flour in my whole-wheat bread, as in the recipe for Golden Wheat Bread (page 85), this recipe is for those of you who like a denser, heavier loaf containing 100 percent of the wheat kernel.

	REGULAR LOAF	LARGE LOAF
Water	⅓ cup	½ cup
Milk	¾ cup	1 cup
Unsalted butter	3 tablespoons	4 tablespoons
Salt	1 teaspoon	1¼ teaspoons
Honey	3 tablespoons	4 tablespoons
Whole-wheat flour	3⅓ cups	4½ cups
Dry yeast	2¼ teaspoons	1 tablespoon
	12 slices	*16 slices*

1. All ingredients must be at room temperature. Liquid ingredients should be approximately 80 degrees F. Cut butter into small cubes. Add ingredients in the order specified in your bread machine owner's manual. Do not use delay bake function.

2. Select whole-wheat or basic bread and normal or medium crust.

3. Remove baked loaf from pan at the end of the baking cycle and cool on a wire rack at least one hour before slicing.

Approximate nutritional analysis per slice: 162 calories, 5 g protein, 27 g carbohydrates, 4 g fiber, 4 g fat, 9 mg cholesterol, 39 mg potassium, 187 mg sodium.

Baker's Note

After removing the bread from the pan, rub a tablespoon of cold butter over the top and sides of the hot loaf as it cools.

• • • •

Apple-Walnut Wheat Bread

THE IS A NICE COUNTRY-INSPIRED loaf, the sort of bread you would expect to find sitting on the rack of a small town bakery. I especially like the rich flavor of the molasses and chewy bits of apples and nuts.

	REGULAR LOAF	LARGE LOAF
Water	¾ cup	1 cup
Egg white, extra-large	1	2
Unsalted butter	2 tablespoons	3 tablespoons
Ground cinnamon	1 teaspoon	1½ teaspoons
Grated nutmeg	¼ teaspoon	½ teaspoon
Salt	1½ teaspoons	2 teaspoons
Molasses	3 tablespoons	4 tablespoons
Whole-wheat flour	¾ cup	1⅓ cups
Bread flour	2¼ cups	2⅔ cups
Dry yeast	2¼ teaspoons	2¼ teaspoons
Chopped, dried apples	½ cup	⅔ cup
Chopped walnuts, lightly toasted	⅓ cup	½ cup
	12 slices	*16 slices*

1. All ingredients must be at room temperature. Liquid ingredients should be approximately 80 degrees F. Cut butter into small cubes. Add ingredients in the order specified in your bread machine owner's manual. Do not use delay bake function. Apples and walnuts can be added 5 minutes before the end of the final kneading cycle.

2. Select whole-wheat or basic bread and normal or medium crust.

3. Remove baked loaf from pan at the end of the baking cycle and cool on a wire rack at least one hour before slicing.

Approximate nutritional analysis per slice: 167 calories, 5 g protein, 28 g carbohydrates, 2 g fiber, 5 g fat, 5 mg cholesterol, 132 mg potassium, 280 mg sodium.

Baker's Note

After removing the bread from the pan, rub a tablespoon of cold butter over the top and sides of the hot loaf as it cools.

Whole-Wheat Date-Nut Bread

WHEN WORKING ON THIS RECIPE, I wanted something a bit different from the basic fruit-and-nut bread. Remembering how I always enjoy the rich, sweet flavor of traditional date-nut bread, I began experimenting until I came up with this yeast-bread version, made with 100 percent whole-wheat flour and buttermilk. Try this bread with a thick smear of cream cheese.

	REGULAR LOAF	LARGE LOAF
Water	½ cup	⅔ cup
Buttermilk	¾ cup	1 cup
Unsalted butter	2 tablespoons	3 tablespoons
Salt	1 teaspoon	1½ teaspoons
Brown sugar	2 tablespoons	3 tablespoons
Whole-wheat flour	3⅓ cups	4½ cups
Dry yeast	2¼ teaspoons	1 tablespoon
Chopped, pitted dates	½ cup	⅔ cup
Chopped walnuts, lightly toasted	⅓ cup	½ cup
	12 slices	*16 slices*

1. All ingredients must be at room temperature. Liquid ingredients should be approximately 80 degrees F. Cut butter into small cubes. Add ingredients in the order specified in your bread machine owner's manual. Do not use delay bake function. Dates and walnuts can be added 5 minutes before the end of the last kneading cycle.

2. Select whole-wheat or basic bread and normal or medium crust.

3. Remove baked loaf from pan at the end of the baking cycle, and cool on a wire rack at least one hour before slicing.

Baker's Note

After removing the bread from the pan, rub a tablespoon of cold butter over the top and sides of the hot loaf as it cools.

Approximate nutritional analysis per slice: 183 calories, 6 g protein, 30 g carbohydrates, 5 g fiber, 5 g fat, 6 mg cholesterol, 106 mg potassium, 196 mg sodium.

Basic Whole-Wheat Pastry Dough

WHOLE-WHEAT FLOUR IS NOT generally recommended for making pastries. The simple reason is that it is high in gluten, the natural protein that makes bread chewy, a characteristic not associated with good pastries. I found, however, that if combined with plain yogurt, the gluten relaxes, resulting in a very soft, tender, almost flaky, pastry dough.

You can use this dough to make an endless variety of sweet breads and rolls as given on the following pages, or use it to make any of the pull-apart breads on pages 81 to 83. You can even shape it into dinner rolls, following the instructions on pages 69 to 75.

¼ cup water
1 extra-large egg
¾ cup plain yogurt
2 tablespoons unsalted butter
¾ teaspoon salt
2 tablespoons brown sugar
2½ cups bread flour
1 cup whole-wheat flour
2¼ teaspoons dry yeast

1, All ingredients must be at room temperature. Liquid ingredients should be approximately 80 degrees F. Cut butter into small cubes. Add ingredients in the order specified in your bread machine owner's manual. Do not use delay bake function.

2. Select manual/dough.

3. At the end of the program, punch down the dough with your knuckles. Let dough rest 5 minutes.

4. Proceed with any of the recipes on pages 97 to 100.

Sweet or Savory Butterhorns

THESE ARE SO GOOD! They're easy to make, look like they came from your local bakeshop, and taste, well, just let me say a batch doesn't last more than a couple of hours at our home. The sweet version, filled with brown sugar and nuts, makes a great Danishlike bun to serve with coffee or tea. The savory butterhorns are chockful of minced onion and hundreds of crunchy seeds; our favorite is poppy, but the choice is up to you.

---

1 recipe Basic Whole-Wheat Pastry Dough, page 96

6 tablespoons unsalted butter, softened

FOR SWEET BUTTERHORNS:

¼ cup packed brown sugar

¼ cup finely chopped walnuts

½ teaspoon ground cinnamon

FOR SAVORY BUTTERHORNS:

6 tablespoons finely minced onion

6 tablespoons sesame or poppy seeds, or a combination

1 extra-large egg, beaten with 1 teaspoon water (egg wash)

Makes 16 butterhorns

1. Divide dough in half. Roll into 12-inch circles. Spread each with half the butter. Combine filling ingredients and sprinkle each circle with half the mixture.

2. Cut each circle into 8 equal wedges. To shape, begin at wide edge and roll toward point. Pinch point to center, so that the butterhorn does not unravel during baking. Bend into a half-moon shape, and place on two large, greased baking pans. Cover and let rise 45 minutes to 1 hour, or until doubled in bulk.

3. Preheat oven to 375 degrees F. Brush butterhorns with egg wash and bake 12 to 15 minutes, or until golden brown.

continued on next page

Sweet or Savory Butterhorns (*cont.*)

4. Remove from oven and cool on a wire rack. Serve warm.

Approximate nutritional analysis per Sweet Butterhorn: 176 calories, 5 g protein, 22 g carbohydrates, 2 g fiber, 8 g fat, 32 mg cholesterol, 63 mg potassium, 149 mg sodium.

Approximate nutritional analysis per Savory Butterhorn: 177 calories, 6 g protein, 21 g carbohydrates, 2 g fiber, 9 g fat, 32 mg cholesterol, 68 mg potassium, 148 mg sodium.

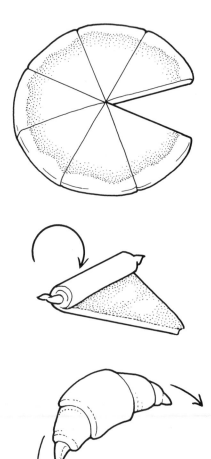

Coconut-Pecan Coffee Cake

DO YOU REMEMBER pecan rings made from rich Danish dough and drizzled with icing, sold at most bakeshops? Well, I've made it even better, by using my recipe for tender whole-wheat pastry dough and adding flaky, moist coconut to the filling. The only thing I eliminated were the pecans on top which, for some reason, always seemed to disappear, leaving tell-tale pock marks in the icing! The results are so good that I am certain that this coffee cake will soon become a personal favorite at your house, too.

1 recipe Basic Whole-Wheat Pastry Dough, page 96
6 tablespoons unsalted butter, softened
⅓ cup packed brown sugar
½ teaspoon ground cinnamon
½ cup flaked coconut
½ cup finely chopped pecans
1 extra-large egg beaten with 1 teaspoon water (egg wash)

16 slices

ICING:

½ cup confectioners' sugar
¼ teaspoon vanilla extract
2 teaspoons warm water

1. Roll dough out into a 24 x 8-inch rectangle. Spread butter over top of dough, ½ inch from edges. Combine filling ingredients and sprinkle on dough.

2. Roll up tightly, jelly-roll fashion, pinching long seam closed. Form into an oval pinching the two ends together. Place on a lightly greased, large baking pan. Cut at 1-inch intervals with a very sharp knife, three-quarters of the way through, so that dough remains attached at the center, fanning slices open slightly so that they lie on their side, overlapping each other.

3. Cover and let rise 45 minutes to an hour, or until doubled in bulk.

continued on next page

Coconut-Pecan Coffee Cake (*cont.*)

4. Preheat oven to 375 degrees F. Brush the coffee cake with egg wash and bake 15 to 20 minutes, or until golden brown.

5. Remove from oven and cool on a wire rack. Combine icing ingredients and drizzle on cooled cake.

Approximate nutritional analysis per slice: 224 calories, 5 g protein, 28 g carbohydrates, 2 g fiber, 11 g fat, 47 mg cholesterol, 85 mg potassium, 161 mg sodium.

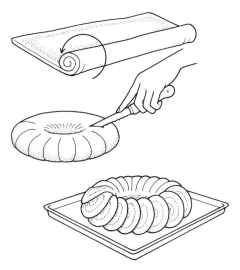

A HARDY, DISEASE-RESISTANT PLANT, RYE HAS BEEN valued by Europeans for making bread for hundreds of years. In fact, in countries like Finland and Sweden where growing seasons are short, rye is milled into flour and made into round flatbreads with holes in the center, stored on poles for eating during the long, cold winters.

Fortunately for us, our European ancestors brought their rye seeds and bread recipes with them. Since rye is relatively low in gluten, it has to be mixed with high-gluten wheat flour. Other

Spanning the Globe with Rye Bread

flavors like fragrant caraway or fennel seeds and grated orange peel are sometimes added to make these breads even more complex in flavor, as you will see in the following recipes.

Good Old New York Deli Rye

NEW YORK IS KNOWN FOR its mile-high deli sandwiches of corned beef and pastrami, and New Yorkers know good rye bread. Slightly chewy with a certain tartness to it, this traditional rye has now been adapted for the bread machine.

	REGULAR LOAF	LARGE LOAF
Water	¾ cup	¾ cup
Buttermilk	½ cup	⅔ cup
Unsalted butter	2 tablespoons	3 tablespoons
Salt	1 teaspoon	1½ teaspoons
Dark-brown sugar	1 tablespoon	4 teaspoons
Caraway seeds	2 teaspoons	1 tablespoon
Coarse ground cornmeal	2 tablespoons	3 tablespoons
Bread flour	2 cups	2⅔ cups
Medium- or whole-grain rye flour	1 cup	1⅓ cups
Dy yeast	2¼ teaspoons	2¼ teaspoons
	12 slices	*16 slices*

1. All ingredients must be at room temperature. Liquid ingredients should be approximately 80 degrees F. Cut butter into small cubes. Add ingredients in the order specified in your bread machine owner's manual. Do not use delay bake function.

2. Select whole wheat or basic bread and normal or medium crust.

3. Remove baked loaf from pan at the end of the baking cycle, and cool on a wire rack at least one hour before slicing.

Approximate nutritional analysis per slice: 125 calories, 4 g protein, 22 g carbohydrates, 2 g fiber, 3 g fat, 6 mg cholesterol, 66 mg potassium, 190 mg sodium.

Swedish *Limpa* Rye

LIMPA, A CLASSIC RYE BREAD FROM SWEDEN, is fragrant with molasses, spices, and orange peel. This is the perfect bread to slice very thin, spread with a little sweet butter, and serve with smoked salmon or a good farmhouse cheese.

	REGULAR LOAF	LARGE LOAF
Water	1 cup	1 cup
Unsalted butter	3 tablespoons	4 tablespoons
Salt	1½ teaspoons	2 teaspoons
Dark brown sugar	2 tablespoons	3 tablespoons
Molasses	2 tablespoons	3 tablespoons
Grated orange zest	1 tablespoon	1 tablespoon
Caraway seeds	½ teaspoon	¾ teaspoon
Fennel seeds	½ teaspoon	¾ teaspoon
Ground cumin	½ teaspoon	¾ teaspoon
Bread flour	2 cups	2⅔ cups
Medium or stone-ground rye flour	1 cup	1⅓ cups
Dry yeast	2¼ teaspoons	1 tablespoon
Raisins, optional	¼ cup	⅓ cup
Golden raisins, optional	¼ cup	⅓ cup
	12 slices	*16 slices*

1. All ingredients must be at room temperature. Liquid ingredients should be approximately 80 degrees F. Cut butter into small cubes. Add ingredients in the order specified in your bread machine owner's manual. Do not use delay bake function. Raisins may be added 5 minutes before the end of the last kneading cycle.

continued on next page

Swedish *Limpa* Rye (*cont.*)

2. Select sweet or basic bread and normal or medium crust.

3. Remove baked loaf from pan at the end of the baking cycle and cool on a wire rack at least one hour before slicing.

Approximate nutritional analysis per slice: 161 calories, 4 g protein, 30 g carbohydrates, 2 g fiber, 3 g fat, 8 mg cholesterol, 154 mg potassium, 271 mg sodium.

St. Paddy's Day Rye

THIS RYE HAS GREAT, intense flavor, from the addition of dark beer and sauerkraut. This is my all-time-favorite loaf to serve on St. Paddy's Day with thick slices of corned beef, wedges of boiled cabbage, and hot, spicy horseradish mustard.

	REGULAR LOAF	LARGE LOAF
Dark beer	¾ cup	1 cup
Unsalted butter	2 tablespoons	3 tablespoons
Salt	1 teaspoon	1½ teaspoons
Molasses	3 tablespoons	5 tablespoons
Sauerkraut, drained	¼ cup	½ cup
Caraway seeds	½ teaspoon	¾ teaspoon
Dried dillweed	2 teaspoons	1 tablespoon
Bread flour	2 cups	2⅔ cups
Medium or stone-ground rye flour	1 cup	1⅓ cups
Dry yeast	2¼ teaspoons	2¼ teaspoons
	12 slices	*16 slices*

1. All ingredients must be at room temperature. Liquid ingredients should be approximately 80 degrees F. Cut butter into small cubes. Add ingredients in the order specified in your bread machine owner's manual. Do not use delay bake function.

2. Select basic or whole-wheat cycle and normal or medium crust.

3. Remove baked loaf from pan at the end of the baking cycle and cool on a wire rack at lest one hour before slicing.

Approximate nutritional analysis per slice: 131 calories, 4 g protein, 25 g carbohydrates, 2 g fiber, 2 g fat, 4 mg cholesterol, 123 mg potassium, 199 mg sodium.

Baker's Note

After removing the bread from the pan, rub a tablespoon of cold butter over the top and sides of the hot loaf as it cools.

Rye Sour Starter

SOME OF THE BEST rye breads are made from a rye sour starter. Although it requires a bit more work, for those who enjoy a full-flavored, dense rye, it pays off in the flavor and texture of the bread. Begin preparing the starter 36 to 48 hours before you plan to use it.

2¼ teaspoons dry yeast
1½ cups water
2 cups medium or stone-ground rye flour
1 tablespoon caraway seeds
1 medium onion, coarsely chopped, tied in a piece of cheesecloth

Makes approximately 3 cups

1. Combine yeast, water, rye flour, and caraway seeds in a clean plastic or glass 4-quart container. When well mixed, push onion bundle into center of mixture with a spatula. Cover tightly with plastic wrap, and let stand in a warm place 24 hours.

2. Remove and discard onion. Use rye sour starter to make Old Milwaukee Sourdough Rye Bread (page 107), or store in a clean glass jar in the refrigerator.

3. To use refrigerated sour starter, measure out the amount specified in the recipe. Let starter come to room temperature, approximately 4 hours.

4. To replenish rye sour, add 3 parts rye flour to 2 parts water and 1 teaspoon sugar. Stir into existing starter and let stand in a warm place 10 to 12 hours. Sour will rise and become bubbly. Stir down and store in the refrigerator.

5. If you do not use your rye sour starter every week, stir in 1 teaspoon of sugar to maintain it and keep it active. It can be stored indefinitely as long as it is replenished once a week.

Old Milwaukee Sourdough Rye Bread

IT IS ONLY FITTING that this rye bread be named for Milwaukee, a city well-known for its hearty German and Slavic cooking, thanks to a large population of Central and Eastern European descent.

	REGULAR LOAF	LARGE LOAF
Water	½ cup	¾ cup
Egg, extra-large	1	1
Unsalted butter	2 tablespoons	3 tablespoons
Salt	1½ teaspoons	2 teaspoons
Molasses	4 teaspoons	2 tablespoons
Rye sour starter, page 106	¾ cup	1 cup
Caraway seeds	2 teaspoons	1 tablespoon
Medium or stone-ground rye flour	¾ cup	1 cup
Bread flour	2¼ cups	3 cups
Dry yeast	2¼ teaspoons	1 tablespoon
	12 slices	*16 slices*

1. All ingredients must be at room temperature. Liquid ingredients should be approximately 80 degrees F. Cut butter into small cubes. Add ingredients in the order specified in your bread machine owner's manual. Do not use delay bake function.

2. Select basic or whole-wheat cycle and normal or medium crust.

3. Remove baked loaf from pan at the end of the baking cycle, and cool on a wire rack at least one hour before slicing.

Approximate nutritional analysis per slice: 130 calories, 4 g protein, 22 g carbohydrates, 2 g fiber, 3 g fat, 26 mg cholesterol, 78 mg potassium, 186 mg sodium.

Baker's Note

After removing the bread from the pan, rub a tablespoon of cold butter over the top and sides of the hot loaf as it cools.

Russian Black Bread

TRADITIONALLY THE BREAD of the Russian working class, black breads are dense, fragrant, and chewy with a coarse texture, especially if prepared using stone-ground rye flour.

	REGULAR LOAF	LARGE LOAF
Water	⅔ cup	1 cup
Buttermilk	½ cup	⅔ cup
Dark molasses	2 tablespoons	3 tablespoons
Unsalted butter	2 tablespoons	3 tablespoons
Salt	1½ teaspoons	2 teaspoons
Onion powder	1½ teaspoons	2 teaspoons
Caraway seeds, crushed	2 teaspoons	3 teaspoons
Fennel seeds, crushed	½ teaspoon	¾ teaspoon
Instant coffee granules	1½ teaspoons	2 teaspoons
Unsweetened cocoa	4 teaspoons	2 tablespoons
Bread flour	2 cups	2½ cups
Medium or stone-ground rye flour	1 cup	1½ cups
Dry yeast	2¼ teaspoons	1 tablespoon
	12 slices	*16 slices*

1. All ingredients must be at room temperature. Liquid ingredients should be approximately 80 degrees F. Cut butter into small cubes. Add ingredients in the order specified in your bread machine owner's manual. Do not use delay bake function.

2. Select basic or whole-wheat cycle and normal or medium crust.

3. Remove baked loaf from pan at the end of the baking cycle, and cool on a wire rack at least one hour before slicing.

Baker's Note

After removing the bread from the pan, rub a tablespoon of cold butter over the top and sides of the hot loaf as it cools.

Approximate nutritional analysis per slice: 132 calories, 4 g protein 25 g carbohydrates, 2 g fiber, 3 g fat, 6 mg cholesterol, 130 mg potassium, 281 mg sodium.

Variations: Add dried currants, raisins, or chopped prunes, ½ cup for a regular loaf, and ⅔ cup for a large loaf, 5 minutes before the end of the last kneading cycle.

Pumpernickel Roll-Up Sandwich

THIS BREAD IS A MEAL in itself, with ham and cheese rolled up in tangy, dark pumpernickel bread, richly flavored with mustard and caraway seeds. Try substituting smoked turkey breast and Muenster cheese for the ham and Swiss.

½ cup water
½ cup buttermilk
2 tablespoons dark molasses
2 tablespoons vegetable oil
1½ teaspoons salt
1½ teaspoons onion powder
2 teaspoons caraway seeds, crushed
1 teaspoon mustard seeds
1½ teaspoons instant coffee granules
4 teaspoons unsweetened cocoa
2 cups bread flour
1 cup medium or stone-ground rye flour
2¼ teaspoons dry yeast

FILLING:
¼ pound Black Forest or smoked Virginia ham, sliced thin
¼ pound imported Swiss cheese, shredded

TOPPING:
1 extra-large egg white, beaten with a teaspoon of water
2 tablespoons sesame seeds

16 slices

1. All ingredients must be at room temperature. Liquid ingredients should be approximately 80 degrees F. Add ingredients in the order specified in your bread machine owner's manual.

2. Select manual/dough.

3. At the end of the program, punch down the dough. Let dough rest 5 minutes.

4. Lightly grease a large baking pan.

5. Lightly dust work surface with flour. Roll the dough into a 16- x 12-inch rectangle. Sprinkle with the shredded Swiss cheese, 1 inch from the edges, and cover with the sliced ham.

6. Starting with the long side, roll up jelly-roll fashion into a tight cylinder. Pinch the seam together as well as the ends. Tuck the ends under. Carefully place on the baking pan. Cover and let rise 45 minutes to 1 hour, or until double in bulk.

7. Preheat even to 400°F.

8. Bake 25 to 30 minutes.

9. Cool on a wire rack before slicing.

Approximate nutritional analysis per slice: 148 calories, 7 g protein, 18 g carbohydrates, 2 g fiber, 5 g fat, 25 mg cholesterol, 137 mg potassium, 407 mg sodium.

IT WAS NOT TOO LONG AGO THAT, WHEN YOU WENT TO buy a loaf of bread, your options were limited to white, wheat, rye, and, perhaps, Italian. Nowadays, your options are endless, with breads ranging from country-style loaves chock-full of healthy seeds and nuts, to European peasant breads and sophisticated variations made with olives, tomatoes, and herbs. But rather than pay upward of five dollars for a loaf of bread, you can now make these breads for your family and friends with in-

Breads with a Flair

gredients readily available in most supermarkets, at a fraction of the cost.

Basic European White Bread

THIS VERY BASIC, simple bread can either be made from start to finish in the bread machine, or can be hand shaped into baguettes or rolls. The addition of rye flour gives the bread the extra chew and crisper crust associated with European-style loaves.

	REGULAR LOAF	LARGE LOAF
Water	1 cup	1⅓ cups
Olive oil	4 teaspoons	2 tablespoons
Salt	1 teaspoon	1½ teaspoons
Sugar	1 teaspoon	1 teaspoon
Medium rye flour	2 tablespoons	3 tablespoons
Bread flour	3 cups	4 cups
Dry yeast	2¼ teaspoons	2¼ teaspoons
	12 slices	*16 slices*

1. All ingredients must be at room temperature. Liquid ingredients should be approximately 80 degrees F. Add ingredients in the order specified in your bread machine owner's manual.

2. Select basic or French cycle and normal or medium crust.

3. Remove baked loaf from pan at the end of the baking cycle, and cool on a wire rack at least one hour before slicing.

Approximate nutritional analysis per slice: 119 calories, 4 g protein, 22 g carbohydrates, 1 g fiber, 2 g fat, 0 mg cholesterol, 15 mg potassium, 179 mg sodium.

Semolina Bread with Toasted Sesame Seeds

SEMOLINA IS COARSELY GROUND flour milled from hard durum wheat. With a distinctive golden color, it is too coarse to be used alone in making bread, and must be blended with white bread flour. Its bright yellow color and nutty flavor shines through, however, especially when combined with toasted sesame seeds.

	REGULAR LOAF	LARGE LOAF
Water	1 cup	1⅓ cups
Olive oil	4 teaspoons	2 tablespoons
Salt	1 teaspoon	1½ teaspoons
Sugar	1 teaspoon	1 teaspoon
Lightly toasted sesame seeds	⅓ cup	½ cup
Finely ground semolina flour	⅔ cup	1 cup
Bread flour	2⅓ cups	3 cups
Dry yeast	2¼ teaspoons	2¼ teaspoons
	12 slices	*16 slices*

1. All ingredients must be at room temperature. Liquid ingredients should be approximately 80 degrees F. Add ingredients in the order specified in your bread machine owner's manual.

2. Select basic or French cycle and normal or medium crust.

3. Remove baked loaf from pan at the end of the baking cycle, and cool on a wire rack at least one hour before slicing.

Approximate nutritional analysis per slice: 149 calories, 5 g protein, 24 g carbohydrates, 1 g fiber, 4 g fat, 0 mg cholesterol, 47 mg potassium, 179 mg sodium.

Black-Olive-and-Rosemary Bread

OVER THE PAST FEW YEARS wonderful, innovative, peasant-type breads have been created by a new generation of bread bakers. One of my favorite loaves is the one that follows. As a lover of olives in any shape or size, I particularly enjoy the slightly bitter taste of cured black olives, with the resinous undertone of fresh rosemary, two very distinct flavors from the sun-bleached hills of the Mediterranean region.

	REGULAR LOAF	LARGE LOAF
Water	1¼ cups	1½ cups
Olive oil	1 tablespoon	4 teaspoons
Salt	1 teaspoon	1½ teaspoons
Whole-wheat flour	½ cup	⅔ cup
Bread flour	2½ cups	3⅓ cups
Dry yeast	2¼ teaspoons	2¼ teaspoons
Oil-cured black olives, pitted	½ cup	¾ cup
Fresh rosemary, coarsely chopped	2 tablespoons	3 tablespoons
	12 slices	*16 slices*

Variation: Toasted walnuts can add interesting texture to this bread. If desired, add ⅓ cup coarsely chopped walnuts for regular loaf, and ½ cup for a large loaf 5 minutes before the end of the final kneading cycle.

1. All ingredients must be at room temperature. Liquid ingredients should be approximately 80 degrees F. Add ingredients in the order specified in your bread machine owner's manual. Olives and rosemary can be added 5 minutes before the end of the last kneading cycle.

2. Select basic or French cycle and normal or medium crust.

3. Remove baked loaf from pan at the end of the baking cycle and cool on a wire rack at least one hour before slicing.

Approximate nutritional analysis per slice: 131 calories, 4 g protein, 22 g carbohydrates, 2 g fiber, 3 g fat, 0 mg cholesterol, 12 mg potassium, 248 mg sodium.

Chewy Country Bread with Seeds

IT WAS A BRIGHT, SUNNY, February morning a couple of years ago. We had just arrived in Amsterdam for a long weekend of sightseeing, when we stumbled across an outdoor market located on a side street between two canals. While intrigued with the diverse offerings ranging from herring to contraband videos, what I will always remember most was the sight and taste of the breads, especially a very chewy peasant loaf chockfull of seeds. It was so simple, yet so flavorful and delicious. I am pleased to have been able to come up with this recipe to share with you.

	REGULAR LOAF	LARGE LOAF
Water	1¼ cups	1½ cups
Olive oil	4 teaspoons	2 tablespoons
Honey	1 tablespoon	4 teaspoons
Salt	1½ teaspoons	2 teaspoons
Lightly toasted sesame seeds	¼ cup	⅓ cup
Poppy seeds	2 tablespoons	3 tablespoons
Raw pumpkin seeds	¼ cup	⅓ cup
Rye flour	¼ cup	⅓ cup
Whole-wheat flour	¼ cup	⅓ cup
Bread flour	2½ cups	3⅓ cups
Dry yeast	2¼ teaspoons	2¼ teaspoons
	12 slices	*16 slices*

Approximate nutritional analysis per slice: 151 calories, 5 g protein, 22 g carbohydrates, 2 g fiber, 6 g fat, 0 mg cholesterol, 68 mg potassium, 269 mg sodium.

1. All ingredients must be at room temperature. Liquid ingredients should be approximately 80 degrees F. Add ingredients in the order specified in your bread machine owner's manual.

2. Select basic or French cycle and normal or medium crust.

3. Remove baked loaf from pan at the end of the baking cycle and cool on a wire rack at least one hour before slicing.

Tomato-and-Basil Bread

THIS IS A FANTASTIC LOAF, fragrant with tomatoes and basil. It develops a thick crust and chewy crumb, and is perfect for serving with vine-ripened tomatoes and fresh mozzarella drizzled with extra-virgin olive oil. I also like to use this bread to make *Panzanella,* a Tuscan bread salad (page 190).

	REGULAR LOAF	LARGE LOAF
Tomato juice	1 cup	1⅓ cups
Olive oil	4 teaspoons	2 tablespoons
Fresh basil, chopped	¼ cup	⅓ cup
Salt	½ teaspoon	¾ teaspoon
Sugar	1½ teaspoons	1½ teaspoons
Medium rye flour	2 tablespoons	3 tablespoons
Bread flour	3 cups	4 cups
Dry yeast	2¼ teaspoons	2¼ teaspoons
	12 slices	*16 slices*

1. All ingredients must be at room temperature. Liquid ingredients should be approximately 80 degrees F. Add ingredients in the order specified in your bread machine owner's manual.

2. Select basic or French cycle and normal or medium crust.

3. Remove baked loaf from pan at the end of the baking cycle, and cool on a wire rack at least one hour before slicing.

Approximate nutritional analysis per slice: 123 calories, 4 g protein, 23 g carbohydrates, 1 g fiber, 2 g fat, 0 mg cholesterol, 64 mg potassium, 163 mg sodium.

Pesto-and-Toasted-Walnut Bread

PESTO IS AN AROMATIC, fresh herb sauce from Italy, usually made from basil, garlic, pine nuts, Parmesan cheese, and extra-virgin olive oil. Relatively unknown here until a few years ago, we have readily accepted and adapted it for many uses, including with pasta, grilled chicken and in bread, both for flavor and color. When making this bread, I like adding toasted walnuts, which seem to highlight pesto's complex flavors as well as adding interesting texture.

Either prepare pesto using a favorite recipe, or purchase it in small jars at specialty-food stores or containers in the refrigerator case of most supermarkets, alongside fresh pasta.

	REGULAR LOAF	LARGE LOAF
Water	1 cup	1¼ cups
Pesto	⅓ cup	½ cup
Salt	¾ teaspoon	1¼ teaspoons
Sugar	¾ teaspoon	1 teaspoon
Whole-wheat flour	¼ cup	½ cup
Bread flour	2¾ cups	3½ cups
Dry yeast	2¼ teaspoons	2¼ teaspoons
Toasted, finely chopped walnuts	⅓ cup	½ cup
	12 slices	*16 slices*

1. All ingredients must be at room temperature. Liquid ingredients should be approximately 80 degrees F. Add ingredients in the order specified in your bread machine owner's manual. Walnuts can be added 5 minutes before the end of the last kneading cycle.

2. Select basic or French cycle and normal or medium crust.

3. Remove baked loaf from pan at the end of the baking cycle, and cool on a wire rack at least one hour before slicing.

Approximate nutritional analysis per slice: 123 calories, 4 g protein, 21 g carbohydrates, 1 g fiber, 3 g fat, 0 mg cholesterol, 29 mg potassium, 134 mg sodium.

French Bread

FRENCH BREAD, OR *BAGUETTES,* as we have learned to call them, are long, narrow loaves of bread with a thin crisp crumb and chewy crust, traditionally made with white flour and perhaps a bit of rye for strength. I also enjoy making baguettes using other adaptable doughs, and recommend that you try making them using any of the following recipes.

One regular loaf recipe:

Basic European White Bread, page 113;

Semolina Bread with Toasted Sesame Seeds, page 114;

Black-Olive-and-Rosemary Bread, page 115; or

Tomato-and-Basil Bread, page 117

Cornmeal for dusting pan

Makes two baguettes, *12 slices each*

1. Prepare dough. All ingredients must be at room temperature. Liquid ingredients should be approximately 80 degrees F. Add ingredients in the order specified in your bread machine owner's manual.

2. Select manual/dough.

3. At the end of the program, punch down the dough. Let dough rest 5 minutes.

4. Lightly sprinkle a large baking pan with fine cornmeal.

5. Lightly dust work surface with flour. Cut dough into 2 equal pieces. With a floured rolling pin, roll each piece into a 10-x-6-inch rectangle.

6. Fold dough in half lengthwise. With the side of your hand, form a crease down center of dough. Fold dough over crease. Securely pinch the seam together to form a tight log.

continued on next page

7. Stretch *baguette* until it is approximately 11 inches long, by rolling it back and forth a few times, working it from the center out to the ends as you stretch it, so that the ends wind up narrower than the center.

8. Carefully place baguettes on prepared baking pan. Let rise, covered, 45 minutes to 1 hour, or until they have doubled in bulk.

9. Preheat oven to 450 degrees F. With a razor blade or a very sharp knife, slash each *baguette* 4 or 5 times diagonally on top. Mist or brush with water.

10. Place baking pan in bottom third of oven. Place 4 ice cubes on the bottom of the oven to create steam. Close the door at once, and bake 20 to 30 minutes, or until golden brown in color and crust is very crisp when squeezed.

11. Cool baked loaves on a wire rack.

Approximate nutritional analysis per slice when made with Basic European White Bread: 60 calories, 2 g protein, 11 g carbohydrates, 1 g fiber, 1 g fat, 0 mg cholesterol, 8 mg potassium, 90 mg sodium.

Approximate nutritional analysis per slice when made with Semolina Bread with Toasted Sesame Seeds: 75 calories, 3 g protein, 12 g carbohydrates, 1 g fiber, 2 g fat, 0 mg cholesterol, 24 mg potassium, 90 mg sodium.

Approximate nutritional analysis per slice when made with Black-Olive-and-Rosemary Bread: 66 calories, 2 g protein, 11 g carbohydrates, 1 g fiber, 2 g fat, 0 mg cholesterol, 6 mg potassium, 124 mg sodium.

Approximate nutritional analysis per slice when made with Tomato-and-Basil Bread: 123 calories, 4 g protein, 23 g carbohydrates, 1 g fiber, 2 g fat, 0 mg cholesterol, 64 mg potassium, 163 mg sodium.

Banneton

A *BANNETON* IS A CLOTH-LINED, woven basket used by French bakers when rising dough; it gives the loaf a distinct design and shape. This method is easily adapted for home baking by using a 10-inch round or oval straw or wicker breadbasket dusted with flour. As the ball of dough rises, it takes on the woven design of the basket, making for an attractive, country loaf. This simple-to-use method is perfect for achieving professional-looking results without hand shaping the dough.

One large loaf recipe:
Basic European White Bread, page 113;
Semolina Bread with Toasted Sesame Seeds, page 114;
Black-Olive-and-Rosemary Bread, page 115; or
Tomato-and-Basil Bread, page 117
Cornmeal and all-purpose flour for dusting

Makes one loaf, 16 slices

1. Prepare dough. All ingredients must be at room temperature. Liquid ingredients should be approximately 80 degrees F. Add ingredients in the order specified in your bread machine owner's manual. Any whole ingredients like nuts or seeds can be added 5 minutes before the end of the last kneading cycle.

2. Select manual/dough.

3. At the end of the program, punch down the dough. Let dough rest 5 minutes.

4. Heavily dust inside of basket with flour. Press dough into basket. Let rise, covered, 45 minutes to 1 hour, or until doubled in bulk.

5. Preheat oven to 450 degrees F.

continued on next page

Banneton (cont.)

6. Lightly sprinkle a large baking pan with fine cornmeal. Turn basket with risen dough over on to baking pan. Remove basket without disturbing shape of dough.

7. Place baking pan in bottom third of oven. Place 4 ice cubes on the bottom of the oven to create steam. Close door at once and bake 40 to 45 minutes, or until golden brown.

8. Cool baked loaf on a wire rack.

Approximate nutritional analysis per slice when made with Basic European White Bread: 119 calories, 4 g protein, 22 g carbohydrates, 1 g fiber, 2 g fat, 0 mg cholesterol, 15 mg potassium, 179 mg sodium.

Approximate nutritional analysis per slice when made with Semolina Bread with Toasted Sesame Seeds: 149 calories, 5 g protein, 24 g carbohydrates, 1 g fiber, 4 g fat, 0 mg cholesterol, 47 mg potassium, 179 mg sodium.

Approximate nutritional analysis per slice when made with Black-Olive-and-Rosemary Bread: 131 calories, 4 g protein, 22 g carbohydrates, 2 g fiber, 3 g fat, 0 mg cholesterol, 12 mg potassium, 248 mg sodium.

Approximate nutritional analysis per slice when made with Tomato-and-Basil Bread: 123 calories, 4 g protein, 23 g carbohydrates, 1 g fiber, 2 g fat, 0 mg cholesterol, 64 mg potassium, 163 mg sodium.

Partybrot

I FIRST DISCOVERED THIS interesting-looking bread on a trip to Switzerland. A large, round loaf made up of many small rolls, *partybrot* is a specialty of Swiss-German bakers.

Easy to assemble, this is a perfect bread to make for a party, and is especially attractive when two or more different types of dough are used, especially when they complement each other in color, texture, and taste. All of the bread doughs in this chapter combine well with each other, so the choice is yours. After making the first batch of dough, place it in a large, greased mixing bowl. Cover the top of the bowl tightly with plastic wrap, and place in the refrigerator, so that the dough rises slowly. Serve the loaves whole, to be pulled apart when served.

---

1 regular loaf recipe of two different breads from this chapter:

Basic European White Bread, page 113;

Semolina Bread with Toasted Sesame Seeds, page 114;

Black-Olive-and-Rosemary Bread, page 115 or;

Tomato-and-Basil Bread, page 117

3 tablespoons seeds, such as sesame, poppy, or caraway, for sprinkling

---

Makes two loaves, or 26 rolls

1. Prepare dough. All ingredients must be at room temperature. Liquid ingredients should be approximately 80 degrees F. Add ingredients in the order specified in your bread machine owner's manual. Any whole ingredients, such as nuts or seeds, can be added 5 minutes before the end of the last kneading cycle.

2. Select manual/dough.

3. At the end of the program, punch down dough. Let dough rest 5 minutes.

4. Lightly grease 2 9-inch round baking pans.

continued on next page

5. Remove first batch of dough from refrigerator, and punch down until it deflates.

6. Lightly dust work surface with flour. Shape each batch of dough into a 13-inch-long cylinder. Cut each cylinder into 1-inch pieces and shape into balls.

7. Place one ball in center of each pan. Place six balls of dough, alternating flavors, around the center ball. Space evenly.

8. Place another six balls of dough around perimeter of pan in between the center ring of balls.

9. Cover and let rise 45 minutes to 1 hour, or until doubled in bulk.

10. Preheat oven to 425 degrees F. Mist or brush tops of rolls with water. Sprinkle with seeds.

11. Place baking pans in bottom third of oven. Place 4 ice cubes on the bottom of the oven to create steam. Close the door at once and bake 30 to 35 minutes, or until golden brown in color.

12. Cool baked loaves on a wire rack.

Approximate nutritional analysis per roll made with Semolina Bread with Toasted Sesame Seeds and Black-Olive-and-Rosemary Bread: 140 calories, 5 g protein, 2 g fiber, 4 g fat, 0 mg cholesterol, 30 mg potassium, 213 mg sodium.

Dutch-Crunch Dinner Rolls

YOU HAVE PROBABLY SEEN Dutch-Crunch Dinner Rolls, chewy white rolls with thick, crackled tops, in your local bakery many times without knowing what they are. A delicious taste sensation, these balls of dough are dipped into a mixture made from rice flour that, when baked, cracks into golden brown, crisp pieces of thick crust.

---

1 regular loaf recipe of Basic European White Bread, page 113

DUTCH CRUNCH TOPPING:

2 tablespoons active dry yeast

2½ teaspoons sugar

¼ teaspoon salt

6 tablespoons rice flour (available in health food stores, do not use sweet rice flour)

1 teaspoon vegetable oil

⅓ cup lukewarm water

Makes 12 rolls

1. Prepare dough. All ingredients must be at room temperature. Liquid ingredients should be approximately 80 degrees F. Add ingredients in the order specified in your bread machine owner's manual.

2. Select manual/dough.

3. At the end of the program, punch down the dough. Let dough rest 5 minutes.

4. Lightly grease a large baking pan.

5. Lightly dust work surface with flour. Shape the dough into a 12-inch-long cylinder. Cut cylinder into 1-inch pieces, and shape into smooth balls by stretching the dough out and down a couple of

continued on next page

Dutch-Crunch Dinner Rolls (*cont.*)

times, always pinching together the bottom edges. Place the rolls on the prepared baking pan, cover, and let rise 45 minutes to an hour, or until doubled in bulk.

6. Prepare the Dutch-Crunch Topping in a large mixing bowl. Let sit, covered, 30 minutes, or until doubled in bulk.

7. Preheat oven to 375 degrees F. Beat the topping mixture and carefully dip the risen rolls into the mixture so that the top third gets covered. Space evenly on the baking pan.

8. Place baking pan in bottom third of oven. Place 4 ice cubes on the bottom of the oven to create steam. Close the door at once and bake 20 to 25 minutes, or until golden brown.

9. Cool baked rolls on a wire rack.

Approximate nutritional analysis per roll: 148 calories, 5 g protein, 27 g carbohydrates, 2 g fiber, 2 g fat, 0 mg cholesterol, 44 mg potassium, 224 mg sodium.

ALL PROFESSIONAL CHEFS AND BAKERS HAVE SIGNATURE recipes, which are usually their most popular and requested recipes. If I had to choose one yeast dough recipe to be this book's signature recipe, it would, without a doubt, be the one for classic *brioche* dough and everything I can do with it! You see, with this wonderful, easy-to-work-with yeast dough, I can perform magic in my kitchen and transform it into the world's best jelly doughnuts, a fabulous, fresh-fruit kuchen, or even classic

Just Like from the Pastry Shop

American sticky buns, all of which look and taste just like they came from a pastry shop!

Classic *Brioche* Dough

A FRENCH TRADITION, *brioche* is a light yeast-risen bread made with eggs and butter. It is one of my favorite doughs to work with, since I can use it for making an endless variety of baked goods, as you will see.

Although this recipe might seem to contain an excessive amount of fat, in reality it has less fat than, say, short dough or pie crust, while providing more dough to work with. The butter has to be added to the dough gradually, so that it blends in well, and the dough develops a smooth and not-too-sticky consistency.

Since the dough is too soft to work with right from the bread machine, it will need a cold rise, which means that it has to chill at least 12 hours in the refrigerator, so plan accordingly. As you will see, the time and effort are surely worth it!

⅓ cup milk
3 extra-large eggs
12 tablespoons unsalted butter, softened
½ teaspoon salt
4 tablespoons sugar
1¾ cups all-purpose flour
1½ cups bread flour
2¼ teaspoons dry yeast

1. All ingredients must be at room temperature. Liquid ingredients should be approximately 80 degrees F. Cut butter into tablespoons. Add ingredients in the order specified in your bread machine owner's manual, adding just 4 tablespoons of butter to start. Do not use delay bake function.

2. Select manual/dough.

3. Add the remaining butter during the first kneading, 2 tablespoons at a time after the dough comes together in a ball.

4. At the end of the program, punch down dough. Let dough rest 5 minutes.

5. Butter a 3-quart bowl. Place dough in bowl, cover tightly with plastic wrap and refrigerate. Refrigerate 12 to 24 hours.

6. After the cold rise, proceed with any of the recipes that follow, pages 130 to 150.

Brioches à Tête

BRIOCHES ARE TRADITIONALLY BAKED in individual, small, fluted molds or a large, round loaf. A ball of dough is placed in the mold with a smaller dough ball placed on top, as if it were a body with a head. In fact, the name for this shape is *brioche à tête,* which literally translates as "brioche with a head." Broiche molds are inexpensive and are available at most housewares stores. You can also use a muffin pan, although you won't have the distinctive fluted edges.

Warm *brioches à tête* are delicious served with fruit preserves for breakfast, along with a steaming cup of café au lait.

1 recipe chilled Classic *Brioche* Dough, page 128
2 tablespoons unsalted butter, softened
1 extra-large egg yolk, beaten with 1 tablespoon milk (egg wash)

Makes 10 brioches à tête

1. Grease the sides and bottoms of 10 individual brioche molds, 3 inches in diameter, with the butter. If using a muffin pan, butter 10 cups.

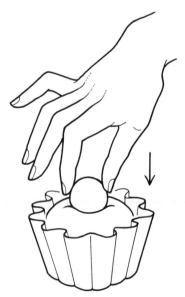

2. Lightly dust work surface with flour. Punch down the cold dough and divide into 10 equal pieces.

3. Take ¾ of 1 piece of dough, and form it into a smooth ball. Place it in a prepared *brioche* mold or muffin cup. Press down in the center with your thumb to make a ½-inch-deep indentation. Roll the remaining small piece of dough into a ball. Wet the bottom of the ball in the egg wash and place in the indentation on top of the larger ball. Repeat with the remaining dough. If using *brioche* molds, place on a 13-x-9-inch baking pan. Cover the *brioche* with a clean kitchen cloth and let rise 1 to 1½ hours, or until doubled in bulk.

4. Preheat the oven to 375 degrees F.

5. Lightly brush the *brioche* with egg wash, and place in the center of the oven to bake 15 to 20 minutes, or until golden brown.

6. Cool on a wire rack 5 minutes before unmolding. Unmold and serve warm, or cool to room temperature before serving.

Approximate nutritional analysis per *Brioche*: 340 calories, 8 g protein, 35 g carbohydrates, 1 g fiber, 19 g fat, 139 mg cholesterol, 80 mg potassium, 137 mg sodium.

Sticky Buns

OKAY, I'LL ADMIT IT, I am addicted to these sticky buns. It's so bad that I begin giving them away as soon as they are cool enough to handle. That way, I avoid eating more than my fair share.

I think what makes them so special is the glaze. It is made with honey, and has just the right amount of butter in it: not too much, not too little. I'll let you be the judge and, remember, don't say that I didn't warn you.

---

1 recipe chilled Classic *Brioche* Dough, page 128

FILLING:

¾ cup light-brown sugar, packed

1 teaspoon ground cinnamon

¼ cup raisins

GLAZE:

1 cup light-brown sugar, packed

¼ cup honey

2 tablespoons unsalted butter

¼ cup chopped walnuts

1 tablespoon water

Makes 24 sticky buns

---

1. Prepare filling by combining ingredients in a small mixing bowl. Set aside.

2. Lightly grease two 12-cup muffin pans.

3. Prepare glaze by combining the ingredients in a small saucepan. Heat over low heat and simmer, while stirring, 5 minutes. Spoon about 1 tablespoon glaze into each muffin pan cup.

4. Lightly dust work surface with flour. Divide dough into two equal pieces and roll each piece into an 18-x-10-inch rectangle.

5. Sprinkle filling mixture on chilled dough. Starting with the long side, roll up jelly-roll fashion into a tight cylinder. Pinch seam together. Cut cylinders in half, then into 6 equal slices. Put slices in muffin cups. Cover and let rise 45 minutes to 1 hour, or until doubled in bulk.

6. Preheat oven to 375 degrees F.

7. Place muffin pans on large baking pans and place in the center of the oven. Bake 15 to 20 minutes, or until the tops are golden brown.

8. Remove from oven and invert buns onto the baking pan. Spoon any spilled syrup over them. Best served warm.

Approximate nutritional analysis per sticky bun: 395 calories, 7 g protein, 56 g carbohydrates, 1 g fiber, 17 g fat, 98 mg cholesterol, 154 mg potassium, 122 mg sodium.

Danish *Kringle*

WHILE SOME CITIES are known for their monuments, museums, or picturesque avenues, Racine, Wisconsin has the distinction of being known for its ethnic pastry, *kringle*. *Kringle* was brought to Racine at the turn of the century by Danish immigrants who settled in the area. The original *kringles* were made with a heavy crust and usually filled with almond paste, weighing in some cases as much as forty pounds. Today's version is lighter, made with buttery pastry filled with fruit or nuts and covered with a sugar-icing glaze. My version of this delicious, Scandinavian coffee cake is filled with apples.

---

1 recipe chilled Classic *Brioche* Dough, page 128

FILLING:

2 20-oz. cans strained apple-pie filling

1 tablespoon freshly squeezed lemon juice

½ teaspoon ground cinnamon

2 tablespoons unsalted butter, melted, for brushing on *kringle*

GLAZE:

1 cup confectioners' sugar, sifted

2 tablespoons hot water

½ teaspoon vanilla extract

Makes 1 kringle, 18 slices

1. Lightly dust work surface with flour. Roll dough into a 24-x-8-inch-long rectangle.

2. Combine filling ingredients in a large mixing bowl.

3. Lightly butter a large baking pan. Preheat oven to 400 degrees F.

4. Sprinkle filling mixture down center of dough.

5. Fold one long side of dough over the filling, then fold the other side over, overlapping approximately 1½ inches. Pinch edge and ends together to seal.

6. Place *kringle* on prepared baking pan, seam side down, in the shape of a horseshoe. Cover and let rise 45 minutes to 1 hour, or until doubled in bulk.

7. Brush with melted butter. Place in center of oven and bake 15 to 20 minutes, or until golden brown.

8. Remove from pan and cool on wire rack covered with a clean kitchen cloth.

9. Combine glaze ingredients in a small mixing bowl. Glaze while still warm.

Approximate nutritional analysis per slice: 271 calories, 4 g protein, 42 g carbohydrates, 1 g fiber, 10 g fat, 66 mg cholesterol, 72 mg potassium, 103 mg sodium.

The World's Best Jelly Doughnuts

ORIGINALLY FROM GERMANY, where they are aptly called *berliners*, jelly doughnuts are now as American as apple pie. You will be surprised how simple they are to make, and how much better they taste than the commercially available variety. When fried at the right temperature, these are as light as air and never greasy. And, remember, nothing beats the taste of a warm, homemade jelly doughnut.

1 recipe chilled Classic *Brioche* Dough, page 128

FILLING:
¼ cup red raspberry or currant jelly
1 extra-large egg

2 quarts vegetable oil, for frying

COATING:
1 cup granulated sugar

Makes approximately 15 jelly doughnuts

1. Lightly dust work surface with flour. Roll dough into a 16-inch circle, approximately ¼ inch thick.

2. Using 3-inch-round biscuit or cookie cutter, cut out as many rounds as possible. Place on a baking sheet. Gather the scraps, reroll, and cut. You should have about 30 rounds (you will always need an even number of rounds; reroll the dough scraps only once).

3. Spoon ½ teaspoon jelly in the center of half the rounds. Beat egg in a small bowl with a tablespoon of water. Using a pastry brush, brush around jelly to edge of dough with egg wash.

4. Place a plain round on top of each jellied round. Press gently to seal around jelly and edges. Cover and let rise 45 minutes to 1 hour, or until puffed and almost doubled in bulk.

5. Heat 2 inches oil to 360 degrees F in a heavy-bottomed, 3-quart saucepan. Fry 3 doughnuts at a time, 1 to 2 minutes on each side,

or until golden brown. Remove with a slotted spoon and let drain on a wire rack resting on a baking pan. Let oil recover to 360 degrees F before frying the next batch.

6. Roll warm doughnuts in sugar, and cool on a wire rack.

Approximate nutritional analysis per jelly doughnut: 311 calories, 6 g protein, 40 g carbohydrates, 1 g fiber, 15 g fat, 91 mg cholesterol, 58 mg potassium, 97 mg sodium.

Raised Doughnuts and Doughnut Holes

THESE WERE THE FIRST homemade doughnuts I ever made. I remember this because I was surprised how easy they were to make, and how they looked like they were straight out of a bakery window. Originally, I had planned to reroll the doughnut holes, but then decided to fry them up as is, which I think is a great idea since it makes it easy to just pop them in your mouth when no one is looking . . .

DOUGHNUTS:

1 recipe chilled Classic *Brioche* Dough, page 128

2 quarts vegetable oil, for frying

COATING:

1 cup granulated sugar

1 teaspoon ground cinnamon, optional

Makes about 30 raised doughnuts and 30 holes

1. Lightly dust work surface with flour. Roll dough into a 16-inch circle, approximately ¼ inch thick.

2. Using a 3-inch-round doughnut cutter, cut out as many doughnuts as possible. If you do not have a doughnut cutter, use a 3-inch-round biscuit cutter to cut out the doughnuts, and a 1-inch-round cutter to cut out the holes. Place doughnuts and holes on a baking sheet. Gather the scraps once, reroll, and cut.

3. Heat 2 inches oil to 360 degrees F in a heavy-bottomed 3-quart saucepan. Fry 3 doughnuts and a few holes at a time, 1 to 2 minutes on each side, or until golden brown. To get doughnuts to really puff up while frying, dunk them under the oil of couple of times with a slotted spoon.

4. Remove with a slotted spoon and let drain on a wire rack resting on a baking pan. Let oil recover to 360 degrees F before frying the next batch.

5. Roll warm doughnuts and holes in sugar. If desired, mix ground cinnamon with sugar.

Approximate nutritional analysis per raised doughnut and hole: 146 calories, 2 g protein, 18 g carbohydrates, 1 g fiber, 7 g fat, 37 mg cholesterol, 27 mg potassium, 45 mg sodium.

Christmas *Stollen*

GERMANY'S CHRISTMAS YEAST BREAD has, over the years, become an American classic, appearing in almost every bakery from coast to coast.

Stollen is traditionally made with candied fruits like cherries and orange peel. I have updated the standard recipe by substituting chopped dried fruits like apricots, peaches, and apples with excellent results. The ingredients go together quickly, making two full-sized loaves. So simple to make, this is a great bread to give as a holiday gift.

---

1 recipe Classic *Brioche* Dough, page 128, prepared up to step 4; add the dried fruits and nuts

---

⅓ cup dark rum or brandy

---

2 6-oz. packages Sun Maid Dried Fruit Bits

---

grated orange zest from 1 large orange

---

2 tablespoons all-purpose flour

---

1 cup slivered, blanched almonds

TOPPING:

---

6 tablespoons unsalted butter, melted

---

2 tablespoons granulated sugar

½ cup confectioners' sugar

Makes 2 stollen, 12 slices each

1. Soak dried fruits and orange zest in rum while preparing Classic *Brioche* Dough. Sprinkle with flour after one hour.

2. Add dried fruits and almonds to the bread machine, 5 minutes before the end of the last kneading cycle.

3. Butter a 3-quart bowl. Place dough in bowl, cover tightly with plastic wrap, and refrigerate. Punch down after the first hour. Chill an additional 11 hours.

4. Butter a large baking pan.

5. Lightly dust work surface with flour. Divide dough in half and roll each piece into a ¾-inch-thick oval. Brush each oval with melted butter and sprinkle with a tablespoon of granulated sugar. Fold each oval in half lengthwise so that the edges do not meet evenly. Press closed and slide onto prepared baking pan. Brush tops with melted butter and let rise 1 hour, or until doubled in bulk.

6. Preheat oven to 400 degrees F.

7. Brush risen loaves with melted butter and bake 10 minutes. Lower oven temperature to 350 degrees F, and bake an additional 35 to 45 minutes, or until golden brown.

8. Remove and cool on a wire rack. Continue brushing the tops of the *stollen* with melted butter as they cool.

9. Dust with confectioners' sugar when completely cooled.

Approximate nutritional analysis per slice: 238 calories, 4 g protein, 28 g carbohydrates, 2 g fiber, 12 g fat, 54 mg cholesterol, 181 mg potassium, 60 mg sodium.

Fresh Fruit *Kuchen*

THE LAST *KUCHEN* I made is still fresh in my memory. After a couple of days of heavy rain, the sun finally came out and so did our bumper crop of blackberries. Out of nowhere, the bushes were covered with berries, and I picked at least two quarts in less than ten minutes. Since the berries were very juicy and flavorful, I wanted to bake them in something that would absorb all their juices, so off I was to prepare a batch of Classic *Brioche* Dough. The resulting *kuchen* (which is a yeast-raised, fruit-filled or -topped cake) was beyond belief. In fact, this cake represents, in my opinion, the best possible way to showcase summer's sun-ripened fruits: juicy fruit on a base of soft, not-too-sweet cake, perhaps slightly warm from the oven, with a scoop of real vanilla-bean ice cream on top. Try it; I'm sure you'll agree with me.

---

1 recipe chilled Classic *Brioche* Dough, page 128

2 tablespoons unsalted butter, melted

TOPPING:

Approximately 1½ pounds fresh tart apples, apricots, Italian plums, peaches, or berries, such as blackberries, blueberries, or raspberries

½ cup granulated sugar

½ teaspoon ground cinnamon

2 tablespoons unsalted butter, melted

Makes one kuchen, *16 slices*

1. Lightly grease a 15-x-10-x-2-inch baking pan. With fingertips and the heel of your hand, stretch the dough evenly to fit in the pan. Brush lightly with melted butter, cover, and let rise about 45 minutes to 1 hour, or until doubled in bulk.

2. Peel fruit, if desired. Core or pit. Cut into ¼-inch-thick slices, and mix in a large bowl with the sugar and cinnamon. If using berries, add ¼ cup flour to help thicken the juices.

3. Preheat oven to 375 degrees F.

4. Arrange fruit slices in rows on top of risen dough, overlapping slightly (spread berries evenly). Drizzle with remaining melted butter.

5. Bake in center of oven, 30 to 35 minutes, or until golden brown.

Approximate nutritional analysis per slice made with apples: 264 calories, 5 g protein, 32 g carbohydrates, 2 g fiber, 13 g fat, 78 mg cholesterol, 95 mg potassium, 86 mg sodium.

Crumb Buns

WHEN I WAS GROWING UP, Fischer's Bakery was the local meeting place on Sunday mornings. I'll never forget the buns they made, covered with crumbs that would melt in your mouth and confectioners' sugar that would sprinkle all over your chin. If I were lucky, I would get a corner piece, which always seemed to have twice as many crumbs.

Fischer's Bakery is long gone, but the memories aren't. Over the years, I have been working on perfecting my recipe for crumb buns. I think it's now near perfect, but I'll let you decide.

---

1 recipe chilled Classic *Brioche* Dough, page 128

TOPPING:
⅔ cup all-purpose flour
⅓ cup dark-brown sugar, packed
4 teaspoons granulated white sugar
½ teaspoon ground cinnamon
¼ teaspoon grated or ground nutmeg
⅓ cup unsalted butter, softened
¼ cup confectioners' sugar, for dusting

Makes 8 buns

1. Place dough in a greased 13-x-9-inch baking pan. With fingertips and the heel of your hand, stretch the dough evenly in the pan. Cover and let rise about 45 minutes to 1 hour, or until doubled in bulk.

2. Preheat oven to 350 degrees F.

3. Prepare crumb topping by combining all dry ingredients in a medium mixing bowl. Cut in softened butter with two knives, until pea-sized crumbs form.

4. Make indentations with your fingertips into the top of the risen dough, and sprinkle with crumbs.

5. Bake in center of oven, 25 to 30 minutes, or until golden brown.

6. Cool on a wire rack. Dust heavily with confectioners' sugar when cool.

Approximate nutritional analysis per bun: 538 calories, 10 g protein, 62 g carbohydrates, 2 g fiber, 28 g fat, 160 mg cholesterol, 130 mg potassium, 173 mg sodium.

Quick-and-Easy Holiday Breads

WOULDN'T IT BE GREAT to have one quick-and-easy recipe to use over and over again for every holiday on the calendar? The basic *brioche* recipe is just that. By rolling the dough out and trimming it with a pair of kitchen scissors or a knife into different shapes, you can make an endless variety of beautiful holiday breads from Valentine hearts to Easter bunnies to Christmas trees. This is a great "activity" recipe to keep the kids busy; family and friends will be pleased to receive these holiday breads wrapped up in color-cellophane packages.

1 recipe chilled Classic *Brioche* Dough, page 128

TOPPINGS AND DECORATIONS:

1 extra-large egg, beaten with 1 tablespoon water (egg wash)

Candied cherries, raisins, colored sugar, sprinkles

OPTIONAL ICING FOR CHRISTMAS TREES, VALENTINE'S DAY HEARTS, AND ST. PADDY'S DAY SHAMROCKS:

1 cup sifted confectioners' sugar

2 tablespoons hot water

½ teaspoon vanilla extract

Food coloring

Christmas Trees

1. Lightly dust work surface with flour. Divide dough into 3 equal pieces. Roll or pat each piece into a triangle 6 inches across the bottom, and 8 inches long. Place on greased baking pans.

2. With scissors, make 2 diagonal 1-inch-long cuts in base to form trunk. Pull dough away from trunk on each side. Make four diagonal 1-inch cuts on each side to form the branches. Separate slightly. Cover and let rise 45 minutes to 1 hour, or until almost doubled in bulk.

3. Preheat oven to 375 degrees F.

4. Brush the trees with egg wash. Decorate as desired with candied cherries, green sugar, or sprinkles (or bake undecorated, and decorate after baking and cooling with icing and decorations; icing can be colored green by stirring in a few drops of green food coloring).

5. Bake in center of oven 15 to 20 minutes, or until golden brown.

6. Remove from pans and cool on a wire rack.

Makes 3 breads

Approximate nutritional analysis per bread without icing: 1070 calories, 27 g protein, 116 g carbohydrates, 4 g fiber, 56 g fat, 456 mg cholesterol, 275 mg potassium, 476 mg sodium.

Approximate nutritional analysis per bread with icing: 1201 calories, 27 g protein, 149 g carbohydrates, 4 g fiber, 56 g fat, 456 mg cholesterol, 275 mg potassium, 476 mg sodium.

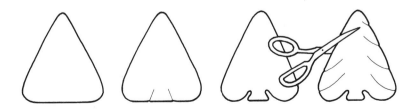

Valentine Hearts

1. Lightly dust work surface with flour. Divide dough into 3 equal pieces. Roll or pat each piece into a triangle 6 inches across the bottom and 8 inches long. Place on greased baking pans.

2. With scissors, make a 2-inch-long straight cut in center of base. Pull dough away from the cut, stretching and tucking it under to form a heart. Cover and let rise 45 minutes to 1 hour, or until almost doubled in bulk.

3. Preheat oven to 375 degrees F.

4. Brush hearts with egg wash. Decorate as desired with chopped or sliced red candied cherries, red sugar, or sprinkles (or bake undecorated, and decorate after baking and cooling with icing and decorations; icing can be colored red or pink by stirring in a couple of drops of red food coloring).

5. Bake in center of oven 15 to 20 minutes, or until golden brown.

6. Remove from pans and cool on a wire rack.

Makes 3 breads

Approximate nutritional analysis per bread without icing: 1070 calories, 27 g protein, 116 g carbohydrates, 4 g fiber, 56 g fat, 456 mg cholesterol, 275 mg potassium, 476 mg sodium.

Approximate nutritional analysis per bread with icing: 1201 calories, 27 g protein, 149 g carbohydrates, 4 g fiber, 56 g fat, 456 mg cholesterol, 275 mg potassium, 476 mg sodium.

St. Paddy's Day Shamrocks

1. Lightly dust work surface with flour. Divide dough into 3 equal pieces. Roll or pat each piece into a triangle 6 inches across the bottom and 8 inches long. Place on greased baking pans.

2. With scissors, make two 2-inch-diagonal cuts in the base for the stem. Pull dough away from stem on each side. Make two inverted, diagonal 1½-inch cuts on each side to form three leaves of shamrock. Pull dough away from cuts, stretching and tucking under, so that it looks like a shamrock. Cover and let rise 45 minutes to 1 hour, or until almost doubled in bulk.

3. Preheat oven to 375 degrees F.

4. Brush shamrocks with egg wash. Decorate shamrocks as desired with chopped green candied cherries or green sugar (or bake undecorated, and decorate as desired after baking and cooling with icing and decorations; icing can be colored green by stirring in a few drops of green food coloring).

5. Bake in center of oven 15 to 20 minutes, or until golden brown.

6. Remove from pans and cool on a wire rack.

Makes 3 breads

Approximate nutritional analysis per bread without icing: 1070 calories, 27 g protein, 116 g carbohydrates, 4 g fiber, 56 g fat, 456 mg cholesterol, 275 mg potassium, 476 mg sodium.

Approximate nutritional analysis per bread with icing: 1201 calories, 27 g protein, 149 g carbohydrates, 4 g fiber, 56 g fat, 456 mg cholesterol, 275 mg potassium, 476 mg sodium.

Easter Bunnies

1. Lightly dust work surface with flour. Shape dough into an 8-inch-long cylinder, then cut into 1-inch pieces. Roll each into an 18-inch-long rope. Cut 10 inches for the body, ½ inch for the tail, and the remaining dough for the head and ears.

2. Coil 10-inch piece of dough for the body and 8-inch piece for the head, leaving 1 inch uncoiled. Place larger of the two coiled rounds (the bunny's body) on a greased baking pan. Make the tail by shaping the ½-inch piece of dough into a small ball. Place at the bottom of bunny's body. Place other coiled round on the baking pan, on top, touching the bunny's body, with uncoiled part on top. Split uncoiled piece of dough in half, down the middle, to form ears. Repeat with remaining dough. Cover and let rise 45 minutes to 1 hour, or until almost doubled in bulk.

3. Preheat oven to 375 degrees F.

4. Brush bunnies with egg wash. Decorate with raisins for eyes and pieces of red candied cherry for mouths.

5. Bake in center of oven 15 to 20 minutes, or until golden brown.

6. Remove from pans and cool on a wire rack.

Makes 8 breads

Approximate nutritional analysis per bread: 401 calories, 10 g protein, 44 g carbohydrates, 2 g fiber, 21 g fat, 171 mg cholesterol, 103 mg potassium, 178 mg sodium.

7 THESE HAVE BEEN MADE AND EATEN AROUND THE WORLD for thousands of years. Today we have come to include these rustic-type breads in our daily diet, either as pizza in its many different forms or sizes, or as the flat breads that we have come to enjoy when making sandwiches or wraps.

These are simple breads that are now even easier to make, using an automatic bread machine. Even the kids can lend a hand in shaping the dough. And, the next time you are short on time and dinner is around the corner, do not forget to look to

Pizza and Flat Breads

your bread machine and the following recipes for quick and easy mealtime inspiration.

Traditional Thin Pizza Crust

OUR LOVE OF PIZZA only seems to grow and grow. With annual sales over $11 billion, what was traditionally an ethnic dish from the Naples region of Italy has become mainstream in less than ninety years. It is no wonder that marketing studies have shown that one of the most popular uses for bread machines after making white bread is making pizza dough. So, begin giving your family and friends a real taste treat and turn out some crisp-crusted, homemade pizzas using your favorite ingredients.

1 cup water
1 tablespoon olive oil
1 teaspoon salt
3 cups bread flour
1½ teaspoons dry yeast

Makes dough for one 16-inch round or 13-x-9-inch rectangular pizza

FLAVORED PIZZA DOUGHS

Whole-Wheat Pizza Crust: Prepare dough according to the recipe, using half whole-wheat flour and half bread flour.

Cheesy Italian-Herb Pizza Crust: Prepare dough according to the recipe, adding 1 teaspoon dried Italian herbs and ¼ cup grated Parmesan or Romano cheese.

South-of-the-Border Pizza Crust: Prepare dough according to the recipe, adding 3 tablespoons cornmeal, and 4 teaspoons prepared taco seasoning mix.

1. All ingredients must be at room temperature. Liquid ingredients should be approximately 80 degrees F. Add ingredients in the order specified in your bread machine owner's manual.

2. Select manual/dough.

3. At the end of the program, punch down the dough. Let dough rest 5 minutes. Proceed with any of the pizza recipes on pages 153 to 156.

Classic Tomato-and-Cheese Pie

THIS RECIPE IS FOR the most commonly eaten version of pizza—plain, with garlicky tomato sauce fragrant with oregano, covered with a stringy layer of mozzarella cheese.

---

1 recipe:

Traditional Thin Pizza Crust, page 152;

Whole-Wheat Pizza Crust, page 152; or

Cheesy Italian-Herb Pizza Crust, page 152

TOPPINGS:

1 (14.5-ounce) can crushed or diced tomatoes

1 tablespoon olive oil

½ teaspoon dried oregano

½ teaspoon dried basil

¼ teaspoon garlic powder

⅛ teaspoon ground black pepper

8 ounces (2 cups) shredded mozzarella cheese

4 teaspoons grated Parmesan or Pecorino Romano cheese

Makes 8 slices

1. In a small saucepan, combine all topping ingredients except the cheeses. Bring to a simmer and cook, covered, 10 minutes.

2. Gently mash cooked tomato sauce against the side of the pot with the back of a mixing spoon to break up any large pieces. Cool to room temperature.

3. Preheat oven to 500 degrees.

4. Lightly oil a 16-inch pizza pan or an 18-x-13-inch baking pan.

continued on next page

Classic Tomato-and-Cheese Pie (*cont.*)

5. Lightly dust ball of dough with flour. With fingertips and heel of your hand, stretch dough evenly in pan.

6. Spread tomato sauce evenly over top of pizza dough. Sprinkle with mozzarella and then grated cheese.

7. Place pan in bottom third of oven and bake 20 to 30 minutes, or until topping is bubbly and bottom is lightly golden.

Approximate nutritional analysis per slice with Traditional Thin Pizza Crust: 280 calories, 12 g protein, 35 g carbohydrates, 2 g fiber, 11 g fat, 23 mg cholesterol, 174 mg potassium, 540 mg sodium.

Approximate nutritional analysis per slice with Whole-Wheat Pizza Crust: 280 calories, 13 g protein, 34 g carbohydrates, 4 g fiber, 11 g fat, 23 mg cholesterol, 174 mg potassium, 540 mg sodium.

Approximate nutritional analysis per slice with Cheesy Italian-Herb Pizza Crust: 294 calories, 13 g protein, 35 g carbohydrates, 2 g fiber, 11 g fat, 25 mg cholesterol, 184 mg potassium, 598 mg sodium.

White Pizza

WE HAVE BEGUN TO ENJOY PIZZA in different guises, like this white version that does not contain any of the traditional tomato sauce. The crust is, instead, covered with five different cheeses and sprinkled with freshly minced parsley.

---

1 recipe:

Traditional Thin Pizza Crust, page 152;

Whole-Wheat Pizza Crust, page 152; or

Cheesy Italian-Herb Pizza Crust, page 152

TOPPINGS:

2 cups (one 15-oz. container) ricotta cheese

2 ounces (½ cup) shredded mozzarella cheese

1 ounce (¼ cup) grated fontina cheese

1 ounce (¼) cup grated provolone cheese

2 tablespoons grated Parmesan cheese

2 tablespoons minced Italian (flat-leaf) parsley

Makes 8 slices

Approximate nutritional analysis per slice with Traditional Thin Pizza Crust: 309 calories, 17 g protein, 34 g carbohydrates, 1 g fiber, 12 g fat, 33 mg cholesterol, 108 mg potassium, 476 mg sodium.

Approximate nutritional analysis per slice with Whole-Wheat Pizza Crust: 309 calories, 17 g protein, 33 g carbohydrates, 3 g fiber, 12 g fat, 33 mg cholesterol, 108 mg potassium, 476 mg sodium.

Approximate nutritional analysis per slice with Cheesy Italian-Herb Pizza Crust: 324 calories, 18 g protein, 34 g carbohydrates, 1 g fiber, 13 g fat, 36 mg cholesterol, 118 mg potassium, 534 mg sodium.

1. Preheat oven to 500 degrees.

2. Lightly oil a 16-inch pizza pan or a large 18-x-13-inch baking pan.

3. Lightly dust ball of dough with flour. With fingertips and heel of your hand, stretch dough evenly in pan.

4. Spread ricotta evenly over top of pizza dough. Sprinkle with remaining ingredients.

5. Place pan with pizza in bottom third of oven and bake 20 to 30 minutes, or until topping is bubbly and bottom is lightly golden.

South-of-the-Border Pizza

SINCE WE HAVE now made pizza our own, why not serve it up south-of-the-border style with salsa and other traditional Tex-Mex adornments?

---

1 recipe for South-of-the-Border Pizza Crust, page 152

TOPPINGS:

2 cups of your favorite brand of prepared salsa

8 ounces (2 cups) shredded Cheddar cheese or taco-blend cheese

½ cup sliced, ripe black olives

3 scallions, trimmed and sliced thin

Makes 8 slices

1. Prepare dough as indicated on page 152.

2. Lightly oil a 16-inch pizza pan or an 18-x-13-inch baking pan.

3. Preheat oven to 500 degrees.

4. Lightly dust the ball of dough with flour. With fingertips and the heel of your hand, stretch the dough evenly in the pan.

5. Spread salsa evenly over top of pizza dough. Sprinkle with remaining topping ingredients.

6. Place pan with pizza in bottom third of oven and bake 20 to 30 minutes, or until topping is bubbly and bottom is lightly golden.

Approximate nutritional analysis per slice with South-of-the-Border Crust: 325 calories, 13 g protein, 39 g carbohydrates, 3 g fiber, 13 g fat, 30 mg cholesterol, 55 mg potassium, 996 mg sodium.

Chicago Deep-Dish Pizza

CHICAGO DEEP-DISH PIZZA combines everything from sausage meat to chopped onions and peppers, bound together with tomato sauce and cheese, and baked in a crust lined pan until everything is hot and bubbly. This is easily a meal in itself.

PIZZA CRUST:
1¼ cups water
2 tablespoons olive oil
½ teaspoon salt
¼ cup grated Parmesan cheese
1 tablespoon cornmeal
3 cups bread flour
2¼ teaspoons dry yeast

TOPPINGS:
2 tablespoons olive oil
1 medium onion, chopped
1 medium green bell pepper, cored, seeded, and diced
8 ounces white mushrooms, sliced thin
16 ounces lean bulk pork sausage or ground beef
2 tablespoons dried Italian herbs
1 14.5-oz. can crushed or diced tomatoes
Salt
Black pepper
8 oz. (2 cups) shredded mozzarella cheese
¼ cup pitted black olives, chopped

Makes 8 slices

continued on next page

Chicago Deep-Dish Pizza (*cont.*)

1. Prepare dough. All ingredients must be at room temperature. Liquid ingredients should be approximately 80 degrees F. Add ingredients in the order specified in your bread machine owner's manual.

2. Select manual/dough.

3. At the end of the program, punch down dough. Let dough rest 5 minutes.

4. Prepare toppings while the bread machine makes the dough.

5. Heat olive oil in a large skillet over medium-high heat and sauté onion, green pepper, and mushrooms until soft. Add meat and cook until no longer pink. Add herbs and tomatoes. Lower to a simmer and cook 15 minutes. Season with salt and pepper to taste. Remove with a slotted spoon to a large mixing bowl, discarding any remaining liquid. Set aside. Stir in the mozzarella and olives when sauce has cooled to room temperature.

6. Preheat oven to 425 degrees F.

7. Lightly grease a 14-inch-round, deep-dish pizza pan or a 13-x 9-x-2-inch baking dish.

8. Lightly dust ball of dough with flour. With fingertips and heel of your hand, stretch dough evenly in pan and at least 2 inches up the sides.

9. Spoon prepared filling onto dough and spread evenly.

10. Place pan with pizza in bottom third of oven and bake 20 to 30 minutes, or until topping is bubbly and edge is golden brown.

Approximate nutritional analysis per slice: 550 calories, 25 g protein, 41 g carbohydrates, 3 g fiber, 32 g fat, 72 mg cholesterol, 569 mg potassium, 1316 mg sodium.

Deep-Dish Taco Bake

SURE TO BE a hit with kids of all ages, this one-pan meal is like a big, soft taco, filled with seasoned ground beef and topped with cheese, lettuce, and tomatoes. Don't forget to serve with your favorite brand of bottled taco sauce.

PIZZA CRUST:

⅔ cup water

2 tablespoons vegetable oil

1 tablespoon sugar

¾ teaspoon salt

1 tablespoon minced onion

½ cup crushed corn or tortilla chips

2 cups bread flour

2¼ teaspoons dry yeast

MEAT FILLING:

2 tablespoons vegetable oil

1 pound lean ground beef

1 medium onion, chopped

1 package taco seasoning mix

¾ cup water

TOPPING:

4 ounces (1 cup) shredded, sharp Cheddar cheese or taco-blend cheese

1 cup shredded leaf lettuce

2 large tomatoes, seeded and coarsely chopped

½ cup sliced black olives

4 scallions, white and light-green parts sliced thin

Bottled taco sauce

Makes 6 servings

continued on next page

Deep-Dish Taco Bake (*cont.*)

1. Prepare dough. All ingredients must be at room temperature. Liquid ingredients should be approximately 80 degrees F. Add ingredients in the order specified in your bread machine owner's manual.

2. Select manual/dough.

3. At the end of the first kneading cycle, press clear/stop.

4. Prepare meat filling while the bread machine makes the crust. Heat oil in a large skillet over medium-high heat. Add ground beef and onion and brown until the meat is no longer pink. Add taco seasoning mix and water. Simmer 25 minutes. Remove from heat and cool to room temperature.

5. Lightly grease a 10-inch pie pan. Scrape prepared dough into pan, forming a rim around the edge. Cover and let rise 20 minutes.

6. Preheat oven to 375 degrees F.

7. Spread taco filling onto dough.

8. Place in oven on center rack. Bake 30 to 35 minutes, or until edge is crisp and lightly golden.

9. Remove from oven, sprinkle top with cheese, lettuce, tomato, black olives, and scallions. Serve hot, with taco sauce.

Approximate nutritional analysis per serving: 697 calories, 25 g protein, 71 g carbohydrates, 7 g fiber, 32 g fat, 91 mg cholesterol, 685 mg potassium, 4581 mg sodium.

Garlic Knots

AVAILABLE AT ALMOST every pizzeria in New York, garlic knots are nothing more than pieces of pizza dough, rolled thin and knotted in the center. After baking they are then dipped in garlic-flavored olive oil. It is amazing how something so simple and easy to make can taste so good! One local pizzeria even turns these savory rolls into miniature sandwiches by slicing them in half and stuffing them with sautéed spinach and shredded mozzarella. Either of the two ways is wonderful!

DOUGH:

1 cup water

2 tablespoons olive oil

1 teaspoon salt

3 cups bread flour

1½ teaspoons dry yeast

GARLIC OLIVE OIL:

½ cup olive oil

6 cloves garlic, peeled and minced

½ teaspoon salt

⅛ teaspoon ground black pepper

SAUTÉED SPINACH AND MOZZARELLA FILLING, OPTIONAL:

1 (10-ounce) package frozen chopped spinach, steamed until just cooked

1 tablespoon olive oil

1 clove garlic, peeled and minced

Salt

1 cup (4 ounces) shredded mozzarella cheese

Makes 12 garlic knots

continued on next page

Garlic Knots (*cont.*)

1. Prepare dough. All ingredients must be at room temperature. Liquid ingredients should be approximately 80 degrees F. Add ingredients in the order specified in your bread machine owner's manual.

2. Select manual/dough.

3. At the end of the program, punch down the dough. Let dough rest 5 minutes.

4. While the bread machine makes dough, prepare garlic olive oil. Combine olive oil, garlic, salt, and black pepper in a small saucepan. Heat over very low heat just until garlic begins to color. Remove from heat and set aside to cool.

5. Prepare spinach, if desired. Squeeze excess liquid from spinach. Heat olive oil over medium-high heat in a small skillet. Add garlic and sauté 1 minute. Add spinach and sauté 2 to 3 minutes, stirring constantly. Season with salt to taste. Set aside, and let cool to room temperature. Add mozzarella, and stir to combine.

6. Lightly oil a large baking pan.

7. Preheat oven to 425 degrees F.

8. Lightly dust work surface with flour. Shape dough into a 12-inch-long cylinder. Cut each cylinder into 1-inch pieces. Roll each piece of dough into an 8-inch rope, ½ inch in diameter. Tie loosely in a knot, leaving two very short ends. Place on the prepared baking pan, cover, and let rise 45 minutes to 1 hour, or until doubled in bulk.

9. Place pan in bottom third of oven and bake 20 to 30 minutes, or until rolls are golden brown.

10. Place on a wire rack to cool 10 minutes.

11. Using kitchen tongs, dip rolls in the garlic olive oil. Let cool on a wire rack 5 minutes before serving.

12. If desired, slice garlic knots almost in half, leaving one side hinged. Fill with sautéed spinach and mozzarella mixture. Place on baking sheet and bake at 375 degrees F, 4 to 5 minutes, or until the cheese is melted. Serve immediately.

Approximate nutritional analysis per Garlic Knot: 202 calories, 4 g protein, 21 g carbohydrates, 1 g fiber, 12 g fat, 0 mg cholesterol, 13 mg potassium, 268 mg sodium.

Approximate nutritional analysis per Garlic Knot with Spinach and Mozzarella: 244 calories, 6 g protein, 22 g carbohydrates, 2 g fiber, 15 g fat, 7 mg cholesterol, 96 mg potassium, 409 mg sodium.

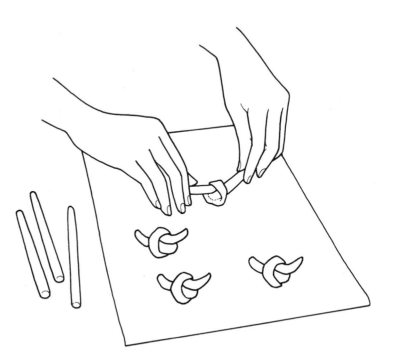

Calzone

WHO SAYS PIZZA has to be round and covered with sauce and cheese? Also originating in Naples, *calzone* is a stuffed pizza made from rounds of yeast dough folded in half and filled with meat or cheese. The name *calzone* reportedly comes from the Italian for "trousers," because these pizzas look like overstuffed pants legs.

DOUGH:
1 cup water
2 tablespoons olive oil
1 teaspoon salt
3 cups bread flour
1½ teaspoons dry yeast

CHEESE FILLING:
2 cups (one 15-oz. container) ricotta cheese
4 ounces (½ cup) shredded mozzarella cheese
¼ cup grated Parmesan or Romano cheese
1 tablespoon minced Italian parsley
12 thin slices pepperoni, optional

Makes 6 calzone

1. Prepare dough. All ingredients must be at room temperature. Liquid ingredients should be approximately 80 degrees F. Add ingredients in the order specified in your bread machine owner's manual.

2. Select manual/dough.

3. At the end of the program, punch down dough. Let dough rest 5 minutes.

4. Prepare filling while the bread machine is making dough. In a medium mixing bowl, combine the filling ingredients, cover, and refrigerate.

5. Grease two large baking pans.

6. Preheat oven to 425 degrees F.

7. Lightly dust work surface with flour. Shape dough into a 6-inch-long cylinder. Cut each cylinder into 1-inch pieces. Dust one piece with flour, and roll out in a ¼-inch-thick circle. Place ⅙ of the cheese-filling mixture in the center of each circle. Top with 2 slices of the pepperoni, if desired.

8. With your fingertip, wet the inside edge of the circle with water. Fold the dough over to make a half-moon, and seal by pinching closed. Fold the edge up and crimp so that the calzone is well sealed. Place on prepared baking pans.

9. Place pans in oven and bake 25 to 30 minutes, or until golden brown. Serve hot.

Approximate nutritional analysis per *calzone*: 393 calories, 20 g protein, 45 g carbohydrates, 2 g fiber, 15 g fat, 34 mg cholesterol, 115 mg potassium, 582 mg sodium.

Basic *Focaccia*

FOCACCIA EMBODIES ALL THE FLAVORS and scents of the Mediterranean kitchen. A coarse, chewy slab of baked bread dough covered with olive oil, coarse salt, and whatever herbs and vegetables there may be on hand, *focaccia* can be as simple or as flavorful as you want it to be.

Focaccia can be cut into small squares and eaten as an accompaniment to a meal, or it can be cut into larger squares, then cut in half to make sandwiches.

DOUGH:
1 cup water
3 tablespoons olive oil
1½ teaspoons salt
3 cups bread flour
2¼ teaspoons dry yeast

BASIC TOPPING:
2 tablespoons extra-virgin olive oil
1 to 2 teaspoons kosher or sea salt

Makes 10 slices

1. Prepare dough. All ingredients must be at room temperature. Liquid ingredients should be approximately 80 degrees F. Add ingredients in the order specified in your bread machine owner's manual.

2. Select manual/dough.

3. At the end of the program, punch down dough. Let dough rest 5 minutes.

4. Lightly oil a 13-x-9-inch baking pan.

5. Lightly dust ball of dough with flour. With fingertips and heel of your hand, stretch dough evenly in pan. Cover and let rise 45 minutes to 1 hour, or until doubled in bulk.

6. Preheat oven to 425 degrees F.

7. Dimple surface of dough with your fingertips, leaving indentations. Drizzle olive oil over surface, making sure that some oil pools in the holes. Sprinkle with desired amount of salt.

8. Place baking pan in bottom third of oven. Place 4 ice cubes on bottom of oven to create steam. Close door at once, and bake 20 to 25 minutes, or until golden brown.

9. Remove immediately from the pan and let cool on a wire rack. Serve warm.

Approximate nutritional analysis per slice: 181 calories, 5 g protein, 25 g carbohydrates, 1 g fiber, 7 g fat, 0 mg cholesterol, 14 mg potassium, 534 mg sodium.

Onion-and-Sage *Focaccia*

THIS *FOCACCIA* RECIPE, from *The Ultimate Bread Machine Cookbook,* received a "seal of approval" from *Good Housekeeping* magazine in their October 1998 issue. The chewy *focaccia* dough is covered with caramelized onions and fragrant, fresh sage leaves making this *focaccia* a personal favorite that I want to share with you once again.

---

1 Recipe Basic *Focaccia,* page 166

TOPPING:

2 large yellow onions, peeled and sliced thin

6 tablespoons extra-virgin olive oil

¼ cup fresh sage leaves

1½ teaspoons kosher salt

Fresh black pepper, coarsely ground

Makes 10 slices

1. Prepare dough as indicated on pages 166 to 167.

2. Sauté sliced onions in 4 tablespoons of oil over low heat in a medium pan until soft and translucent. Do not brown.

3. Lightly oil a 13-x-9-inch baking pan.

4. Lightly dust ball of dough with flour. With fingertips and heel of your hand, stretch dough evenly in pan. Cover and let rise 45 minutes to 1 hour, or until doubled in bulk.

5. Preheat oven to 425 degrees F.

6. Dimple surface of dough with your fingertips, leaving indentations. Spread sautéed onions over surface. Top with fresh sage leaves. Drizzle with remaining two tablespoons of olive oil and sprinkle with salt and black pepper to taste.

7. Place baking pan in bottom third of oven. Place 4 ice cubes on bottom of oven to create steam. Close door at once, and bake 20 to 25 minutes, or until golden brown.

8. Remove immediately from the pan and let cool on a wire rack. Serve warm.

Approximate nutritional analysis per slice: 340 calories, 6 g protein, 45 g carbohydrates, 2 g fiber, 15 g fat, 0 mg cholesterol, 100 mg potassium, 804 mg sodium.

Greek Flat Bread

FLAT BREADS ARE ENJOYED throughout the Mediterranean region, not just in Italy. This example from Greece has a wonderful cheese flavor accented with pungent oregano or mint, two herbs used extensively in classic Greek cooking.

1 cup water
2 tablespoons olive oil
½ teaspoon black pepper
2 teaspoons dried mint or oregano
3 cups bread flour
2¼ teaspoons dry yeast
4 ounces feta cheese, crumbled
1 cup grated Parmesan cheese

TOPPING:

2 tablespoons extra-virgin olive oil

Makes 10 slices

1. All ingredients must be at room temperature. Liquid ingredients should be approximately 80 degrees F. Add ingredients in the order specified in your bread machine owner's manual. Feta and Parmesan cheeses can be added 5 minutes before the end of the last kneading cycle.

2. Select manual/dough.

3. At the end of the program cycle, punch down the dough. Let dough rest 5 minutes.

4. Lightly oil a 13-x-9-inch baking pan.

5. Lightly dust ball of dough with flour. With fingertips and heel of your hand, stretch dough evenly in pan. Cover and let rise 45 minutes to 1 hour, or until doubled in bulk.

6. Preheat the oven to 450 degrees F.

7. Dimple surface of dough with your fingertips, leaving indentations. Brush with olive oil.

8. Place baking pan in bottom third of oven. Place 4 ice cubes on bottom of oven to create steam. Close door at once, and bake 20 to 25 minutes, or until golden brown.

9. Remove immediately from the pan and let cool on a wire rack. Serve warm.

Approximate nutritional analysis per slice: 246 calories, 11 g protein, 25 g carbohydrates, 1 g fiber, 11 g fat, 18 mg cholesterol, 17 mg potassium, 313 mg sodium.

Aladdin's Bread

THIS TRADITIONAL Middle Eastern flat bread is quite simple to prepare. To duplicate the effect of baking the breads directly on the surface of a hot clay oven, we will preheat the metal baking pans before placing the breads on them. You'll be amazed how quickly and how high they puff up.

DOUGH:
1¼ cup water
1½ teaspoons salt
1 teaspoon sugar
3 cups bread flour
2¼ teaspoons dry yeast

TOPPINGS:
1 teaspoon white sesame seeds
1 teaspoon black sesame seeds or poppy seeds

Makes 4 loaves

1. All ingredients must be at room temperature. Liquid ingredients should be approximately 80 degrees F. Add ingredients in the order specified in your bread machine owner's manual.

2. Select manual/dough.

3. At the end of the program, punch down dough. Let dough rest 5 minutes.

4. Divide dough into 4 equal pieces. On a lightly floured work surface, roll dough into an 8-inch round. Brush each round with water, cover, and let rise 30 minutes.

5. Preheat oven to 500 degrees F.

6. Place two large baking pans into the hot oven and heat 10 minutes.

7. Brush dough again with water, and prick several times with a fork. Sprinkle with seeds. Place flat breads on hot baking pans.

8. Place baking pans in oven. Place 4 ice cubes on bottom of oven to create steam. Close door at once, and bake 12 to 15 minutes, or until golden brown.

9. Remove immediately from the pan, and let cool on a wire rack. Serve warm.

Approximate nutritional analysis per loaf: 315 calories, 12 g protein, 63 g carbohydrates, 3 g fiber, 2 g fat, 0 mg cholesterol, 42 mg potassium, 804 mg sodium.

IF YOU HAVE EVER BEEN TO NEW YORK CITY, YOU WILL be familiar with the sight of the pushcart vendors on street corners feeding the masses as they make their way through the city. Although they offer a wide variety of foods ranging from hot dogs with the works, to roasted chestnuts in the fall, some of the most popular foods available are quintessentially New York, including bagels, pretzels, and knishes, all of which can be easily made at home with the help of a bread machine.

Pushcart Breads

Basic Bagel and Pretzel Dough

WHILE DISTINCT IN TASTE and shape, bagels and pretzels are both made from a very similar dough. What distinguishes the two is how the dough is treated prior to baking, as well as their shapes. Nevertheless, both are surprisingly easy to make and, in many cases, are far superior when made at home than what is available commercially. Besides, making homemade bagels or pretzels is a great family activity to occupy a long afternoon.

1½ cups water
1 teaspoon salt
1 tablespoon dark-brown sugar, packed
4 cups bread flour
2¼ teaspoons dry yeast

1. All ingredients must be at room temperature. Liquid ingredients should be approximately 80 degrees F. Add ingredients in the order specified in your bread machine owner's manual.

2. Select manual/dough.

3. At the end of the program, punch down dough. Let dough rest 5 minutes.

4. Proceed with any of the recipes for shaping bagels and pretzels, pages 176 to 180.

Basic Chewy New York–Style Bagels

TRADITIONAL, New York bagels are boiled in water before baking to reduce the starch, producing that classic chewy crust. As simple as this process may seem, it is nearly impossible to achieve at home. I know, I've tried—at least a dozen times. After consulting with the experts, I determined to switch tactics. I made the dough come out as chewy as possible and, to give the bagels a substantial, glossy crust, brushed them with egg wash. The results are near perfect and no one is the wiser!

---

1 recipe Basic Bagel and Pretzel Dough, page 175

½ cup cornmeal for dusting pan

TOPPINGS:

2 extra-large eggs beaten with 1 tablespoon water (egg wash)

Poppy seeds, sesame seeds, coarse kosher salt, finely minced garlic or onions

---

Makes 12 bagels

1. Lightly dust work surface with flour. Shape dough into a 12-inch-long cylinder. Cut into 12 1-inch pieces. Roll each piece into 10-inch-long ropes.

2. Form each rope into a circle, overlapping ends slightly. Fold right end over left end. Tuck under and pinch gently to hold together. Place bagels on baking pans sprinkled with cornmeal. Cover and let rise 30 minutes.

3. Preheat oven to 375 degrees F.

4. Brush top and bottom of bagels with egg wash. Sprinkle top and bottom with toppings, if desired. Let dry on a wire rack 10 minutes.

5. Bake in the center of oven, 15 minutes. Turn over and bake 10 minutes longer, or until golden brown.

6. Cool to room temperature on a wire rack.

Approximate nutritional analysis per plain bagel: 159 calories, 7 g protein, 29 g carbohydrates, 1 g fiber, 2 g fat, 42 mg cholesterol, 36 mg potassium, 192 mg sodium.

Variations:

CINNAMON-RAISIN BAGELS

Add 1 teaspoon ground cinnamon and ½ cup raisins to the Basic Bagel and Pretzel Dough recipe, 5 minutes before the end of the last kneading.

Approximate nutritional analysis per Cinnamon-Raisin Bagel: 180 calories, 7 g protein, 34 g carbohydrates, 2 g fiber, 2 g fat, 41 mg cholesterol, 89 mg potassium, 193 mg sodium.

WHOLE-WHEAT-AND-HONEY BAGELS

Eliminate the brown sugar, and add 3 tablespoons honey to the Basic Bagel and Pretzel Dough recipe. Use 3 cups bread flour and 1 cup whole-wheat flour.

Approximate nutritional analysis per Plain Whole-Wheat-and-Honey Bagel: 172 calories, 7 g protein, 32 g carbohydrates, 2 g fiber, 2 g fat, 41 mg cholesterol, 36 mg potassium, 192 mg sodium.

EGG BAGELS

Reduce water to 1¼ cup and add one extra-large egg to the Basic Bagel and Pretzel Dough recipe.

Approximate nutritional analysis per Egg Bagel: 166 calories, 7 g protein, 29 g carbohydrates, 1 g fiber, 3 g fat, 66 mg cholesterol, 42 mg potassium, 198 mg sodium.

Real German–Style Pretzels

RUMOR HAS IT that the first pretzels were made hundreds of years ago by a diligent, frugal German monk who was also a baker. Tired of discarding his dough scraps, the monk decided to roll them out, and knotted them to resemble hands and arms in prayer.

Delicious and chewy hot from the oven, these pretzels are best when eaten within a couple of hours of baking.

1 recipe Basic Bagel and Pretzel Dough, page 175
½ cup baking soda

TOPPING:

Coarse kosher or sea salt

Makes 12 pretzels

1. Lightly dust work surface with flour. Shape dough into a 12-inch-long cylinder. Cut into 12 1-inch pieces. Roll each piece into 16-inch-long rope.

2. Form each rope into a horseshoe. Cross the ends and twist. Pull ends down and through loops. Pinch to hold shape. Place pretzels on baking pans sprinkled with salt.

3. Preheat oven to 475 degrees F.

4. Bring 2 quarts of water to boil in a 3-quart pot. Add baking soda. Lower to simmer. Place 2 pretzels at a time in the simmering

water for approximately 2 minutes, or until lightly golden. Remove with a slotted spatula to a wire rack sitting over a baking pan. Sprinkle with salt. Let dry 10 minutes. Place on baking pans sprinkled with salt.

5. Place baking pans in center of oven and bake 8 to 10 minutes, or until brown.

6. Cool on a wire rack.

Approximate nutritional analysis per pretzel: 137 calories, 5 g protein, 28 g carbohydrates, 1 g fiber, 1 g fat, 0 mg cholesterol, 15 mg potassium, 1205 mg sodium.

Butter-Dipped Pretzels

PRETZELS LIKE THESE have been appearing in malls from coast to coast for the past few years. They differ from the traditional pushcart pretzel in that they are not boiled, rather they are covered with melted butter before and after baking. Equally delicious, they provide a new twist—no pun intended—especially when sprinkled with different toppings.

---

1 recipe Basic Bagel and Pretzel Dough, page 175

TOPPINGS:

6 tablespoons unsalted butter, melted

Coarse kosher or sea salt, sesame seeds, poppy seeds, cinnamon sugar, or finely crushed almond crunch, for sprinkling on pretzels

---

Makes 12 pretzels

1. Preheat oven to 475 degrees F.

2. Lightly dust work surface with flour. Shape dough into a 12-inch-long cylinder. Cut into 1-inch pieces. Roll each piece into 16-inch-long rope.

3. Form each rope into a horseshoe. Cross ends and twist. Pull the ends down and through the loops. Pinch to hold shape. Place pretzels on buttered baking pans.

4. Generously brush each pretzel with 2 tablespoons melted butter. Sprinkle with toppings, if desired.

5. Place baking pans in center of oven and bake 12 to 14 minutes, or until golden brown.

6. Place on a wire rack over a baking pan. Pour remaining melted butter into a shallow bowl. Dip the baked pretzel in the butter.

7. Cool on a wire rack.

Approximate nutritional analysis per plain Butter-Dipped Pretzel: 170 calories, 5 g protein, 28 g carbohydrates, 1 g fiber, 5 g fat, 10 mg cholesterol, 16 mg potassium, 1205 mg sodium.

Potato Knishes

THE ODDS ARE THAT, if you are not from New York, you have never had a knish. Of Eastern European origin, knishes are potato-filled buns that are chewy on the outside and meltingly delicious on the inside. They are great to serve on a buffet table, or to accompany a bowl of homemade soup on a cool autumn evening.

DOUGH:
¾ cup water
2 tablespoons vegetable oil
1 extra-large egg
½ teaspoon salt
2 teaspoons sugar
3 cups bread flour
1½ teaspoons dry yeast

FILLING:
2 tablespoons vegetable oil
1½ cups minced onion
1½ cups plain mashed potatoes
Salt
Ground black pepper

3 tablespoons vegetable oil, for brushing

Makes 16 knishes

1. Prepare filling by combining ingredients in a large mixing bowl. Add salt and pepper to taste. Cover and set aside.

2. Prepare dough. All ingredients must be at room temperature. Liquid ingredients should be approximately 80 degrees F. Add ingredients in the order specified in your bread machine owner's manual.

continued on next page

Potato Knishes (*cont.*)

3. Select manual/dough.

4. At the end of the program, punch down the dough. Let dough rest 5 minutes.

5. Lightly flour work surface. Roll the dough on a lightly floured surface into a long cylinder, 1½ inches in diameter. Cut into 16 pieces. With your fingers, flatten each piece of dough into a 3-inch round. The edges should be thinner, with a puffy 1-inch center. Place a heaping teaspoon of the filling in the center of the dough and gather the edges together, pressing to seal. Twist gathered edges to prevent them from opening. Repeat with remaining dough and filling.

6. Preheat oven to 350 degrees F.

7. Place the buns, gathered side down, 1 inch apart on an 18-x-12-inch baking pan. Lightly brush with vegetable oil. Cover with a clean cloth and let rise in a warm, draft-free place 15 minutes.

8. Bake 15 to 20 minutes, or until golden brown.

9. Cool on a wire rack. Serve warm.

Approximate nutritional analysis per knish: 161 calories, 4 g protein, 22 g carbohydrates, 1 g fiber, 7 g fat, 16 mg cholesterol, 96 mg potassium, 132 mg sodium.

WHILE HOMEMADE BREAD USUALLY DOES NOT LAST VERY

long, there may be times when you have baked a loaf too many.

Rather than you having the best-fed birds in the neighborhood,

I'll share with you some of my favorite recipes that are great for

cleaning out the breadbox.

Great Things to Make with Leftover Bread

Cinnamon Toast

THERE IS SOMETHING ABOUT CINNAMON TOAST that evokes warm, fuzzy memories from childhood. So much so that a leading cereal company even developed a cinnamon-toast cereal with pieces shaped like small slices of cinnamon-sugar–coated bread. This recipe, though, has got to be one of the easiest ways to prepare toast.

¼ cup sugar, mixed with 1 tablespoon ground cinnamon

8 slices of your favorite bread, toasted

Unsalted butter

Makes 4 servings of 2 slices each

1. Butter hot toast.

2. Sprinkle lightly with cinnamon sugar.

Approximate nutritional analysis per serving made with Homey White Bread: 239 calories, 6 g protein, 39 g carbohydrates, 2 g fiber, 7 g fat, 11 mg cholesterol, 29 mg potassium, 269 mg sodium.

Bread-Pudding Pancakes

WHILE I WAS WORKING ON THIS BOOK, a friend heard me complain about all the leftover day-old bread I was accumulating and came to my rescue with this great breakfast recipe that combines two of my favorites: pancakes and French toast.

¾ cup all-purpose flour
2 tablespoons sugar
1 tablespoon baking powder
7 (½-inch) slices day-old white or wheat bread
2 cups milk
2 extra-large eggs, beaten
3 tablespoons unsalted butter, melted

Makes approximately 10 pancakes

1. Sift together flour, sugar, and baking powder in a medium bowl.

2. Trim crusts from bread and cut into ½-inch pieces.

3. Place bread in a large bowl and cover with milk. Let stand 15 minutes, or until very soft and falling apart.

4. Add flour mixture to bread mixture and stir to blend. Add eggs and melted butter. Let batter sit 15 minutes.

5. Coat a heavy, metal griddle or large skillet with vegetable oil cooking spray. Heat over medium-high heat. Drop batter by ¼ cupfuls onto cooking surface. Cook until bubbles form on surface and pancakes begin to brown, about 2 minutes. Turn and cook on other side until golden, about 2 minutes longer. Remove and repeat with remaining batter. Serve with real maple syrup.

Approximate nutritional analysis per pancake made with Homey White Bread: 144 calories, 6 g protein, 20 g carbohydrates, 1 g fiber, 5 g fat, 50 mg cholesterol, 100 mg potassium, 337 mg sodium.

Caramel-Apple Bread Pudding

THIS IS MY FAVORITE bread pudding. I clipped this recipe out of a local newspaper years ago and, after some revisions, came up with the following version. The brown sugar melts and caramelizes during baking, making a delicious sauce for the apples and pudding. The final result is not too sweet, and leftovers are great for breakfast. Make using white bread or any of your favorite sweet breads like Banana Raisin Oat or Apple Walnut Wheat.

6 tablespoons unsalted butter, softened
1 cup dark brown sugar, packed
1 regular-sized loaf day-old bread, sliced thin
2 Golden Delicious apples, peeled, cored, and sliced thin
3 cups milk
4 extra-large eggs
1 teaspoon vanilla extract
¼ teaspoon salt
1 teaspoon ground cinnamon

Makes 10 servings

1. Butter a 13-x-9-x-2-inch glass baking dish with 2 tablespoons butter. Spread sugar evenly over bottom.

2. Butter bread slices. Layer with apple slices in the pan.

3. In a large mixing bowl, whisk together milk, eggs, vanilla, and salt.

4. Pour on top of bread and apples. Let sit 30 minutes, pressing down with a spatula periodically to wet the top layer of bread. Sprinkle with cinnamon.

5. Preheat oven to 375 degrees F.

6. Bake pudding until the top is puffed and lightly browned, about 1 hour.

7. Let cool on a wire rack 30 minutes to 1 hour. Cut into squares and serve warm.

Approximate nutritional analysis per serving made with Honey White Bread: 351 calories, 11 g protein, 48 g carbohydrates, 2 g fiber, 13 g fat, 124 mg cholesterol, 254 mg potassium, 349 mg sodium.

Strata

THIS IS THE PERFECT brunch dish to prepare when you find you have accumulated odd pieces of bread. For added flavor, try making this with flavorful, savory loaves like Tomato Basil or Onion Poppy Seed.

1 regular loaf of day-old bread, crust removed, cut into ½-inch slices, then 1-inch squares
¾ cup diced boiled or baked ham
2 cups shredded Swiss or sharp Cheddar cheese
⅓ cup snipped chives or thinly sliced scallions, green tops only
6 extra-large eggs
3½ cups milk
½ teaspoon salt
¼ teaspoon ground black pepper
2 tablespoons minced fresh herbs, such as parsley, marjoram, basil, or a combination

Makes 8 servings

1. Butter a 9-x-13-x-2-inch baking dish.

2. Cover the bottom of the baking dish with half the bread squares.

3. Sprinkle with ham, cheese, and chives.

4. Cover with remaining bread.

5. Beat eggs, milk, salt, pepper, and herbs together in a large mixing bowl.

6. Pour over bread. Cover and refrigerate overnight.

7. The next morning, preheat oven to 325 degrees F. Place baking dish on a large baking pan to catch any drips and bake 1 hour, or until puffed and lightly browned.

8. Cut into squares and serve hot or warm.

Approximate nutritional analysis per serving made with Homey White Bread: 373 calories, 22 g protein, 36 g carbohydrates, 1 g fiber, 16 g fat, 217 mg cholesterol, 184 mg potassium, 724 mg sodium.

Tomato and Bread

THIS SUPERB WAY to use stale bread appears in similar guises throughout the Mediterranean region, and the frugal home cook uses what is readily available in abundance: sun-ripened tomatoes, garlic, vibrant extra-virgin oil, and, naturally, day-old bread.

While we are accustomed to ordering the Italian version, *bruschetta,* at restaurants as an appetizer, in Spain, for example, *pan con tomate* is eaten for breakfast with *café con leche.*

Even though this is a very simple dish, you must use day-old bread and the ripest tomatoes possible, otherwise, the results will be dismal and disappointing.

---

4 large slices of bread, such as Basic European White, page 113; Semolina Bread with Toasted Sesame Seeds, page 114; or Tomato-and-Basil Bread, page 117, sliced 1 inch thick

---

1 to 2 large cloves garlic, peeled and cut in half

---

2 medium vine-ripened tomatoes

Extra-virgin olive oil for drizzling

Salt

Makes 4 servings

1. Toast bread on a grill over an open fire or under broiler, until lightly toasted.

2. Rub ½ clove garlic into each slice of toasted bread until it wears down to nothing.

3. The tomato can be prepared two ways: Peel, seed, and cut into ¼-inch cubes. Place evenly over bread slices. Sprinkle with salt, to taste. Drizzle with olive oil. Or, if you prefer, cut tomato in half. Rub tomato half into bread, squeezing slightly, until bread absorbs pulp and juice. Sprinkle with salt and drizzle with olive oil.

Approximate nutritional analysis per serving made with European White Bread:
162 calories, 5 g protein, 27 g carbohydrates, 2 g fiber, 4 g fat, 0 mg cholesterol, 165 mg potassium, 362 mg sodium.

Panzanella

THIS REFRESHING BREAD SALAD from Italy is perfect when served on a hot summer's day with grilled meats or fish. For best results, make this bread salad using day-old slices of European White, Semolina Sesame, or Tomato-and-Basil bread.

2 cups bread, trimmed of crusts, cut into ½-inch cubes and toasted lightly in the oven
3 large vine-ripened tomatoes
¼ cup minced flat-leaf parsley or basil
2 scallions, white and light green parts, trimmed and sliced thin
2 Kirby cucumbers, peeled and cut into ¼-inch cubes
¼ cup extra-virgin olive oil
2 tablespoons red wine vinegar
Salt
Ground black pepper

Makes 4 servings

1. Place the bread in a large mixing bowl.

2. Peel and seed tomatoes. Puree 1 tomato in a food processor and pour over bread. Mix and let sit 15 minutes, or until bread softens.

3. Cut remaining tomatoes into ½-inch pieces. Combine in a serving bowl with remaining ingredients. Add softened bread. Toss to combine. Season with salt and black pepper to taste. Serve at room temperature.

Approximate nutritional analysis per serving made with European White Bread:
196 calories, 3 g protein, 16 g carbohydrates, 2 g fiber, 15 g fat, 1 mg cholesterol, 395 mg potassium, 355 mg sodium.

Salmorejo

WHILE MOST OF US are familiar with *gazpacho,* a cold summertime soup from the south of Spain, you probably have never heard of or eaten *salmorejo,* a thick, creamy, tomato-based soup from the Andalusian city of Córdoba that is prepared and served uncooked. The tomatoes that are used to make the soup have to be extremely ripe, juicy, and flavorful. In order to thicken the soup and give it body, pieces of stale bread are moistened in water and vinegar and added to the tomatoes along with some garlic and olive oil. The resulting soup is thick and creamy, with a rich tomato flavor. As simple as it may seem, the success of this particular recipe lies in the quality of the ingredients and the fact that it is blended for 15 minutes in a food processor.

1 pound (approximately 8 slices) stale bread, such as Homey White Bread (page 36) or Basic European White Bread (page 113), all crusts removed, torn into very small pieces
2 tablespoons white wine or sherry vinegar
Water
1 pound vine-ripened tomatoes, peeled, seeded, and cut into small pieces
1 clove garlic, peeled and quartered
¼ cup extra-virgin olive oil
Salt
2 hard-boiled eggs, sliced thin

Makes 6 servings

1. Place bread in a large mixing bowl. Add vinegar and begin to sprinkle with enough water to moisten; bread should be able to absorb all the water without being very wet. Let sit 10 minutes to soften.

2. Place moistened bread and all remaining ingredients in bowl of a large food processor. Process 15 minutes, or until the mixture is well-blended and creamy.

3. Season with salt to taste.

4. Serve in small bowls with two slices of hard-boiled egg floating on top.

Approximate nutritional analysis per serving: 332 calories, 9 g protein, 44 g carbohydrates, 2 g fiber, 14 g fat, 35 mg cholesterol, 54 mg potassium, 457 mg sodium.

Troubleshooting

For best results in using your bread machine, be sure to read and refer to the Introduction, especially pages 21 to 32, and all the printed instructional materials provided by the bread machine manufacturer.

PROBLEMS:

Bread machine labors during kneading cycle.

Dough does not come together into a ball.

REASON:

Dough is too dry because:
1. Amount of ingredients exceeds manufacturer's recommendations. Check owner's manual for appropriate amount.
2. Recipe contains ingredients that will absorb water if used with delay bake function.
3. Recipe has puréed fruits or vegetables, or whole grains that may require additional water.
4. Water is hard.
5. Eggs smaller than extra-large were used.

SOLUTION:

1. Add additional water, 1 tablespoon at a time, until dough appears smooth and elastic.
2. Use delay bake function only when specified. See Solution 1.
3. See Solution 1.
4. Use bottled water.
5. Only use extra-large eggs.

PROBLEM:

Dough is very sticky.

REASON:

1. Flour has high moisture content.

2. Too much liquid was used.
3. Water is soft.

SOLUTION:

1. Store flour in airtight container, so that it has less chance of absorbing humidity.
2. Add additional flour, 1 tablespoon at a time, until dough appears smooth and elastic.
3. Use bottled water.

PROBLEM:

Dough or bread did not rise enough.

REASON:

1. Ingredients were not at room temperature.
2. Ingredients were not put in the bread pan in the order specified by the manufacturer.
3. Yeast did not activate.
4. Forgot to add yeast.
5. Low-gluten flour was used.
6. High altitude.
7. Hard water.
8. Room temperature was below 68 degrees F.
9. Dough too dry; liquid ingredients not measured accurately.

SOLUTION:

1. Ingredients must be at room temperature, unless otherwise specified.
2. Ingredients must be put in the bread pan in the order specified by the manufacturer.
3. Always check expiration date on back of yeast package. If uncertain as to yeast activity, test yeast as indicated on page 24.
4. Dough and bread will not rise without yeast. Measure and lay out all the ingredients before adding to bread pan to avoid omitting an ingredient.
5. Only use high-gluten bread flour, unless otherwise specified.
6. If baking at an altitude 3,000 feet above sea level, reduce water by 1 tablespoon for every 1,000 feet above 3,000. Do not de-

crease by more than 4 tablespoons. If dough appears to be too dry, add the water, a tablespoon at a time, until the dough appears smooth and elastic.

7. Use bottled water.
8. Only use bread machine in a location that is 68 degrees to 80 degrees F.
9. Use a glass or plastic measuring cup specifically designed for measuring liquids. If recipe calls for eggs, only use extra-large.

PROBLEM:

Dough or bread touches the top of the bread machine lid.

REASON:

1. Weather is very hot and/or humid.
2. Too much yeast was used.

SOLUTION:

1. During periods of high humidity and/or heat, dough may rise too high too quickly. To slow the rising process, use cooler water, approximately 68 degrees F. Another option is to reduce the yeast by approximately ¼ to 1 teaspoon.
2. Be sure to use the amount of yeast specified in the recipe.

PROBLEM:

Bread collapses when baked.

REASON:

Dough rose unevenly, due to:
1. Excess moisture.
2. Too much liquid.
3. High humidity and/or heat can cause dough to rise unevenly.

SOLUTION:

1. Since wheat flour is very absorbent, it can absorb excess moisture during periods of high humidity. Store flour in an airtight container. Try reducing the liquid by 2 to 3 tablespoons.
2. Measure liquid ingredients carefully, using a measuring cup designed for measuring liquids.
3. During periods of high humidity and/or heat, the dough may rise too high too quickly. To slow down the rising process, use cooler water, approximately 68 degrees F. Another option is to reduce the yeast by approximately ¼ to 1 teaspoon.

PROBLEM:

Bread does not bake completely.

REASON:

1. Ingredients not measured properly.
2. Yeast may be old.
3. Bread machine malfunctioning.

SOLUTION:

1. Measure ingredients carefully, using appropriate measuring cups and spoons.
2. Always check expiration date on yeast package. If uncertain as to yeast activity, test yeast as indicated on page 24.
3. Consult bread machine owner's manual; call customer service for advice.

PROBLEM:

Crust too dark or hard.

REASON:

Baking control set too dark.

SOLUTION:

Set the baking control on a lighter setting.

PROBLEM:

Dried fruits and/or nuts are chopped, and do not come out whole.

REASON:

Fruits and/or nuts not added at the appropriate moment, and chopped during the kneading cycle.

SOLUTION:

Add dried fruits and nuts when indicated in the bread machine owner's manual, or five minutes before the end of the final kneading cycle.

PROBLEM:

Dried fruits and/or nuts did not mix in with dough, and wound up on the bottom of the bread pan.

REASON:

They were added too late and did not have sufficient time to be mixed into the dough.

The dough was too dry and inelastic.

SOLUTION:

1. Add ingredients like dried fruits and nuts when indicated in the bread machine owner's manual, or five minutes before the end of the final kneading cycle.
2. Measure liquid ingredients carefully, using a measuring cup designed for measuring liquids. Add additional water, 1 tablespoon at a time, until dough appears smooth and elastic.

Bread Machine and Ingredient Manufacturers

The following bread machine and ingredient manufacturers kindly provided me with samples and/or product information used in developing this cookbook. For your convenience, I have provided the manufacturers' customer-service phone numbers in the event you should have any questions regarding your bread machine or bread machine baking in general. Be sure to have the model and serial number of your bread machine available when calling the manufacturer.

American Harvest: 1-800-288-4545

Betty Crocker: 1-800-688-8782

Black & Decker: 1-800-254-9786

Breadman: 1-888-881-8101, or 1-800-233-9054

Farberware: 1-888-881-8101, or 1-800-233-9054

Fleischmann's Yeast: 1-800-777-4959

Franklin Industries: 1-800-480-2610

General Mills/Gold Medal Flour: 1-800-328-6787

Gold Star: 1-800-243-0000

Hitachi: 1-800-241-6558, or 1-800-448-2244

Magic Chef (model 250-2): 1-888-888-2433

Magic Chef (model ES-1850): 1-800-925-6278

Maxim: 1-888-881-8101, or 1-800-233-9054

Mr. Coffee: 1-800-321-0370

Oster: 1-800-597-5978, or 1-800-526-2832

Panasonic: 1-800-871-5279

Pillsbury Bread Machines: 1-800-858-3277

Pillsbury Flour: 1-800-767-4466

Red Star Yeast: 1-800-445-4746

Regal Ware: 1-800-998-8809

Robin Hood Multifoods (Canada): 1-800-268-3232 (English), or 1-800-363-2756 (French)

Salton: 1-888-881-8101, or 1-800-233-9054

Sanyo: 1-800-421-5013

Sunbeam: 1-800-597-5978

Toastmaster: 1-800-947-3744

Welbilt: 1-800-872-1656

West Bend: 1-800-367-0111

White-Westinghouse: 1-800-245-0600

Zojirushi: 1-800-733-6270

Mail-Order Sources

Although almost all of the ingredients you will ever need to make excellent loaves of quality breads and baked goods are available at your local supermarket, the first two mail-order sources are options for hard-to-find ingredients and supplies. The last two are excellent mail-order sources for gluten-free baking.

King Arthur Flour Baker's Catalog
P.O. Box 876
Norwich, VT 05055
1-800-827-6836

Arrowhead Mills, Inc.
P.O. Box 2059
Hereford, TX 79045
1-800-740-0730

Gluten-Free Pantry
P.O. Box 840
Glastonbury, CT 06033
1-800-291-8386

Ener-G-Foods, Inc.
P.O. Box 84487
Seattle, WA 98124
1-800-331-5222

Index

Aladdin's Bread, 172–73
all-purpose flour, 22
almond(s):
  -and-Cherry Bread, Sweet, 65
  Christmas *Stollen,*140–41
  Pandoro, 78–79
American Harvest, 197
Amy's Bakery (New York City), 43
apple(s):
  Caramel-, Bread Pudding, 186–87
  -Chunk and Walnut Pull-Apart Bread, 82
  Danish *Kringle,* 134–35
  Walnut Wheat Bread, 94
Arrowhead Mills, Inc., 199

bagel(s):
  Chewy New York–Style, Basic, 176–77
  Cinnamon-Raisin, 177
  Dough, Basic, 175
  Egg, 177
  Whole-Wheat-and-Honey, 177
Baguettes (French Bread), 119–20
baking bread, 30–31
  troubleshooting tips for, 195
Banana-Raisin Oat Bread, 89–90
Banneton, 121–22
Barbecued-Pork Buns, Steamed, 52
basil:
  Pesto-and-Toasted-Walnut Bread, 118
  -and-Tomato Bread, 117
    as *Banneton,* 121–22
    as French Bread (*Baguettes*), 119–20
    as *Partybrot,* 123–24

beef, in Deep-Dish Taco Bake, 159–60
Betty Crocker, 197
Black & Decker, 197
Black Bread, Russian, 108–9
Black-Olive-and-Rosemary Bread, 115
  as *Banneton,* 121–22
  as French Bread (*Baguettes*), 119–20
  as *Partybrot,* 123–24
bleached flour, 22
bread:
  in healthful diet, 17–18
  history of, 18
  storing and freezing, 31
bread flour:
  white, 22–23, 35
  whole-wheat, 23
bread machines, 15–32
  appeal of, 18–19
  average purchaser of, 16–17
  flour for, 22–23
  getting best results from, 21–32
  invention of, 15–16
  kids and, 19–20
  liquids for, 25–26
  manufacturers of, 197–98
  measuring ingredients for, 27–28
  mechanics of, 28–29
  price reduction in, 16
  troubleshooting tips for, 32, 192–96
  working with dough from, 29–31
  yeast for, 23–25

Breadman, 197
bread pudding:
  Caramel-Apple, 186–87
  Pancakes, 185
breakfast or brunch fare:
  Bread-Pudding Pancakes, 185
  Brioches à Tête, 130–31
  Caramel-Apple Bread Pudding, 186–87
  Cinnamon Toast, 184
  Jelly Doughnuts, World's Best, 136
  Raised Doughnuts and Doughnut Holes, 138–39
  Sticky Buns, 132–33
  Strata, 188
  Suizos, 76–77
brioche dough:
  Christmas *Stollen,* 140–41
  Christmas Trees, 147
  Classic, 128–29
  Crumb Buns, 144–45
  Danish *Kringle,* 134–35
  Easter Bunnies, 150
  Fresh Fruit *Kuchen,* 142–43
  Holiday Breads, Quick-and-Easy, 146–50
  Jelly Doughnuts, World's Best, 136–37
  Raised Doughnuts and Doughnut Holes, 138–39
  St. Paddy's Day Shamrocks, 149
  Sticky Buns, 132–33
  Valentine Hearts, 148
Brioches à Tête, 130–31
Brownie Bread, Chocolatey Walnut, 41

brunch fare, *see* breakfast or
    brunch fare
bubble breads, *see* pull-apart
    breads
buckwheat flour, 23
Buddha's Delightful Veggie Buns,
    53
bun(s):
    Buddha's Delightful Veggie, 53
    Crumb, 144–45
    Dough, Basic Chinese, 51
    Potato Knishes, 181–82
    Steamed Barbecued-Pork, 52
    Sticky, 132–33
Bunnies, Easter, 150
butter, 26
    -Dipped Pretzels, 180
    measuring, 28
Butterhorns, Sweet or Savory,
    97–98
buttermilk, 26
    White, Old-Fashioned, 38

Calzone, 164–65
candied fruit, Sweet Bread with,
    60
canola oil, 26
Caramel-Apple Bread Pudding,
    186–87
celia sprue disease, 31–32
Challah, 66–67
Cheddar cheese:
    Deep-Dish Taco Bake, 159–60
    -and-herb rolls, 75
    South-of-the-Border Pizza,
    156
    Strata, 188
cheese:
    adding to bread machine, 27
    Calzone, 164–65
    Chicago Deep-Dish Pizza,
    157–58
    Deep-Dish Taco Bake, 159–60
    Greek Flat Bread, 170–71
    -and-Herb Rolls, 75
    Italian-Herb Pizza Crust, 152

Mozzarella and Spinach Filling,
    for Garlic Knots, 161–63
    Pumpernickel Roll-Up Sand-
    wich, 110–11
    South-of-the-Border Pizza, 156
    Strata, 188
    -and-Tomato Pie, Classic,
    153–54
    White Pizza, 155
Cherry-and-Almond Bread,
    Sweet, 65
Chewy Country Bread with
    Seeds, 116
Chicago Deep-Dish Pizza,
    157–58
Chinese bun(s):
    Dough, Basic, 51
    Steamed Barbecued-Pork, 52
    Veggie, Buddha's Delightful, 53
chives, in Herb-and-Cheese Rolls,
    75
chocolate:
    Crumb Pull-Apart Bread,
    Funny as a Monkey, 81
    Walnut-Brownie Bread, 41
Christmas breads:
    Pandoro, 78–79
    Stollen, 140–41
    Sweet, with candied fruit and
    nuts, 60
    Trees, 147
cinnamon:
    -Raisin Bagels, 177
    -Raisin Bread, 42
    -Raisin Whole-Wheat Loaf, 86
    Sweet Butterhorns, 97–98
    Toast, 184
Cloverleaf Rolls, 73–74
coconut:
    -Pecan Coffee Cake, 99–100
    Tropical Hawaiian Bubble
    Bread, 83
coffee cakes:
    Coconut-Pecan, 99–100
    Danish *Kringle,* 134–35
collapsed breads, 194–95

complex carbohydrates, 17
cornmeal:
    Honey Loaf, 43
    Multigrain Bread, 92
corn syrup, 27
Country Bread with Seeds,
    Chewy, 116
cracked wheat, Savory Egg Bread
    with, 56
Cranberry-Orange-Walnut Loaf,
    61
Crumb Buns, 144–45
crusts:
    making chewier and harder,
    30
    troubleshooting tips for,
    195–96
cucumbers, in *Panzanella,* 190
currants:
    Cornmeal Honey Loaf, 43
    Irish Freckle Bread, 44
    Old-Fashioned Oat Bread with,
    46

Danish *Kringle,* 134–35
Date-Nut Whole-Wheat Bread,
    95
Deep-Dish Pizza, Chicago,
    157–58
Deep-Dish Taco Bake, 159–60
Dietary Approaches to Stop Hy-
    pertension (DASH), 17
dinner rolls:
    Basic Dough for, 68
    Cloverleaf, 73–74
    Dutch-Crunch, 125–26
    Fan-Shaped, 71–72
    Herb-and-Cheese, 75
    Parker House, 69–70
doneness, testing for, 30–31
dough:
    storing and freezing, 31
    working with, 29–31
dough conditioners, 23
doughnuts:
    Jelly, World's Best, 136

Raised, and Doughnut Holes, 138–39
dried fruits:
  adding to bread machine, 27
  Christmas *Stollen,* 140–41
  troubleshooting tips for, 196
Dutch-Crunch Dinner Rolls, 125–26

Easter Bunnies, 150
egg(s), 26
  Bagels, 177
  Strata, 188
egg breads, golden, 54–83
  Almond-and-Cherry, Sweet, 65
  Apple-Chunk and Walnut Pull-Apart, 82
  Challah, 66–67
  Chocolate-Crumb Pull-Apart, Funny as a Monkey, 81
  Christmas, 60
  Cloverleaf Rolls, 73–74
  Dinner-Roll Dough, Basic, 68
  Fan-Shaped Rolls, 71–72
  Herb, Fresh, 58
  Herb-and-Cheese Rolls, 75
  Lemon Poppy-Seed Loaf, Glazed, 63–64
  Onion-Poppy-Seed, 57
  Orange-Cranberry-Walnut Loaf, 61
  Pandoro, 78–79
  Parker House Rolls, 69–70
  Pull-Apart Bubble Bread Sweet Dough, Basic, 80
  Pumpkin-Pecan, 62
  Savory, 55–56
  Suizos, 76–77
  Sweet, 59–60
  Tropical Hawaiian Bubble, 83
Ener-G-Foods, Inc., 199
European White Bread, Basic, 113
  as *Banneton,* 121–22
  as French Bread (*Baguettes*), 119–20
  as *Partybrot,* 123–24

Fan-Shaped Rolls, 71–72
Farberware, 197
fat, 26, 30
fennel seeds, in Cornmeal Honey Loaf, 43
fermentation process, 23–24, 25, 26, 27
feta cheese, in Greek Flat Bread, 170
flat breads, 151
  Aladdin's, 172–73
  Focaccia, Basic, 166–67
  Greek, 170–71
  see also pizza
flax seeds:
  Golden Wheat Bread with, 86
  Multigrain Bread, 92
Fleischmann's Yeast, 197
flour, 22–23
  all-purpose, 22
  bleached vs. unbleached, 22
  bread, 22–23, 35
  buckwheat, 23
  measuring, 27
  rye, 23
  semolina, 23
  whole-wheat (graham), 22–23
focaccia:
  Basic, 166–67
  Onion-and-Sage, 168–69
Food Guide Pyramid, 17
Franklin Industries, 197
freezing bread and dough, 31
French breads:
  Banneton, 121–22
  Brioche Dough, Classic, 128–29
  Brioches à Tête, 130–31
  French Bread (*Baguettes*), 119–20
fruit(s):
  adding to bread machine, 27
  candied, Sweet Bread with, 60

dried, in Christmas *Stollen,* 140–41
dried, troubleshooting tips for, 196
Fresh, *Kuchen,* 142–43
see also specific fruits
Funny as a Monkey Chocolate-Crumb Pull-Apart Bread, 81

Garlic Knots, 161–63
General Mills, 197
German breads:
  Christmas *Stollen,* 140–41
  Pretzels, 178–79
glazes, 134–35
  Lemon, 64
gluten, 22, 23, 25, 26, 30
  -free baking, 31–32
Gluten-Free Pantry, 199
golden breads:
  egg, *see* egg breads, golden
  Wheat, 85–86
Gold Medal Flour, 197
Gold Star, 197
Good Old New York Deli Bread, 102
graham flour, *see* whole-wheat (graham) flour
Greek Flat Bread, 170–71

Hagman, Bette, 32
ham:
  Pumpernickel Roll-Up Sandwich, 110–11
  Strata, 188
Hawaiian Bubble Bread, Tropical, 83
healthful diet, 17–18
Hearts, Valentine, 148
herb(s):
  adding to bread machine, 27
  -and-Cheese Rolls, 75
  Fresh, Bread, 58
  Italian-, Pizza Crust, Cheesy, 152
  measuring, 27

Hitachi, 197
holiday breads, 146–50
   Christmas *Stollen,* 140–41
   Christmas Trees, 147
   Easter Bunnies, 150
   icing for, 146
   St. Paddy's Day Rye, 105
   St. Paddy's Day Shamrocks,
     149
   Sweet, with candied fruit and
     nuts, 60
   toppings and decorations for,
     146
   Valentine Hearts, 148
Homey White Bread, 36–37
honey, 26
   Cornmeal Loaf, 43
   measuring, 27–28
   substituting for sugar, 37
   -and-Whole-Wheat Bagels, 177

icing, for holiday breads, 146
ingredients:
   cheese, 27
   fat, 26
   flour, 22–23
   fruits and nuts, 27
   herbs and spices, 27
   liquids, 25–26
   mail-order sources for, 199
   manufacturers of, 197–98
   measuring, 27–28
   salt, 26, 27
   sugar and other sweeteners,
     26–27
   temperature of, 25, 26, 28
   yeast, 23–25
instant-read thermometers, 30
Irish breads:
   Freckle, 44
   St. Paddy's Day Rye, 105
Italian fare:
   Focaccia, Basic, 166–67
   Onion-and-Sage *Focaccia,*
     168–69
   Pandoro, 78–79

Panzanella, 190
see also pizza

Japan, bread machines in, 15–16
jelly:
   Doughnuts, World's Best, 136
   Peanut-Butter-and-, (PBJ)
     Bread, 91

kids, bread machines and, 19–20
King Arthur Flour Baker's Catalog, 199
kitchen scales, digital, 28
kneading, 29
   in bread machine, 25
   gluten and, 22
   troubleshooting tips for, 192
Knishes, Potato, 181–82
Kringle, Danish, 134–35
Kuchen, Fresh Fruit, 142–43

leftover bread, things to make
   with, 183–91
   Bread-Pudding Pancakes, 185
   Caramel-Apple Bread Pudding,
     186–87
   Cinnamon Toast, 184
   Panzanella, 190
   Salmorejo, 191
   Strata, 188
   Tomato and Bread, 189
lemon:
   Glaze, 64
   Poppy-Seed Loaf, Glazed, 63–64
   zest, Sweet Bread with, 60
Limpa Rye, Swedish, 103–4
liquid ingredients, 25–26
   measuring, 28

macadamia nuts, in Tropical
   Hawaiian Bubble Bread, 83
Magic Chef, 197
mail-order sources, 199
maple syrup, 27
   Old-Fashioned Oat Bread with,
     46

margarine, 26
   measuring, 28
Maxim, 197
measuring, 27–28
milk, 25–26
   measuring, 28
millet seeds:
   Golden Wheat Bread with, 86
   Savory Egg Bread with, 56
Mr. Coffee, 197
molasses, 26
   measuring, 27–28
mozzarella cheese:
   Calzone, 164–65
   Chicago Deep-Dish Pizza,
     157–58
   and Spinach Filling, for Garlic
     Knots, 161–63
   Tomato-and-Cheese Pie, Clas-
     sic, 153–54
   White Pizza, 155
Multigrain Bread, 92
mushrooms, in Chicago Deep-
   Dish Pizza, 157–58

National Institutes of Health
   (NIH), 17
New York City breads:
   Chewy Bagels, Basic, 176–77
   see also pushcart breads
nut(s):
   adding to bread machine, 27
   Date-, Whole-Wheat Bread,
     95
   Sweet Bread with, 60
   troubleshooting tips for, 196
   see also specific nuts

oat(s):
   Banana-Raisin Bread, 89–90
   Bread, Old-Fashioned,
     45–46
   Multigrain Bread, 92
oil, 26
   measuring, 28
Ojima, Shin, 15–16

old-fashioned breads:
    Buttermilk White, 38
    Oat, 45–46
Old Milwaukee Sourdough Rye
    Bread, 107
olive(s):
    Chicago Deep-Dish Pizza,
       157–58
    Deep-Dish Taco Bake, 159–60
    -and-Rosemary Bread, 115
       as *Banneton,* 121–22
       as French Bread (*Baguettes*),
          119–20
       as *Partybrot,* 123–24
    South-of-the-Border Pizza, 156
olive oil, 26
100 Percent Whole-Wheat Bread,
    93
onion:
    Chicago Deep-Dish Pizza,
       157–58
    -Poppy-Seed Bread, 57
    -and-Sage *Focaccia,* 168–69
    Savory Butterhorns, 97–98
orange:
    -Cranberry-Walnut Loaf, 61
    zest, in Christmas *Stollen,*
       140–41
    zest, Sweet Bread with, 60
Oster, 197
oven spring, 30

Panasonic, 197
Pancakes, Bread-Pudding, 185
Pandoro, 78–79
Panzanella, 190
Parker House Rolls, 69–70
Parmesan cheese, in Greek Flat
    Bread, 170
Partybrot, 123–24
pastry(ies), 127–50
    Brioche Dough, Classic,
       128–29
    Brioches à Tête, 130–31
    Christmas *Stollen,* 140–41
    Christmas Trees, 147

Coconut-Pecan Coffee Cake,
    99–100
Crumb Buns, 144–45
Danish *Kringle,* 134–35
Easter Bunnies, 150
Fresh Fruit *Kuchen,* 142–43
Jelly Doughnuts, World's Best,
    136
Raised Doughnuts and Dough-
    nut Holes, 138–39
St. Paddy's Day Shamrocks, 149
Sticky Buns, 132–33
Sweet or Savory Butterhorns,
    97–98
Valentine Hearts, 148
Whole-Wheat, Dough, Basic,
    96
PBJ (Peanut-Butter-and-Jelly)
    Bread, 91
peasant-type breads:
    Black-Olive-and-Rosemary, 115
    Chewy Country, with Seeds,
       116
pecan(s):
    -Coconut Coffee Cake, 99–100
    -Pumpkin Bread, 62
    Tropical Hawaiian Bubble
       Bread, 83
peppers, in Chicago Deep-Dish
    Pizza, 157–58
Pesto-and-Toasted-Walnut Bread,
    118
Pillsbury Bread Machines, 197
Pillsbury Flour, 197
pineapple, in Tropical Hawaiian
    Bubble Bread, 83
pizza, 151–65
    Calzone, 164–65
    Chicago Deep-Dish, 157–58
    Deep-Dish Taco Bake, 159–60
    South-of-the-Border, 156
    Tomato-and-Cheese Pie, Clas-
       sic, 153–54
    White, 155
pizza dough:
    Cheesy Italian-Herb Crust, 152

Deep-Dish Crust, 157–58
Garlic Knots, 161–63
South-of-the-Border Crust, 152
taco-style crust, 159–60
Traditional Thin Crust, 152
Whole-Wheat Crust, 152
poppy seed(s):
    Aladdin's Bread, 172–73
    Chewy Country Bread with
       Seeds, 116
    Golden Wheat Bread with, 86
    -Lemon Loaf, Glazed, 63–64
    -Onion Bread, 57
    Savory Butterhorns, 97–98
Pork, Barbecued-, Buns, Steamed,
    52
potato(es):
    Bread, Real Farmhouse, 39–40
    Knishes, 181–82
    Salt-Rising Bread Starter, 49
    water or mashed potatoes, as
       liquid ingredient, 26
    Wheat-Flake Bread, 87–88
pretzel(s):
    Butter-Dipped, 180
    Dough, Basic, 175
    Real German–Style, 178–79
problem solving, *see* troubleshoot-
    ing
pudding(s):
    Bread-, Pancakes, 185
    Caramel-Apple Bread, 186–87
pull-apart (bubble) breads:
    Apple-Chunk and Walnut, 82
    Basic Sweet Dough for, 80
    Chocolate-Crumb, Funny as a
       Monkey, 81
    Tropical Hawaiian, 83
Pumpernickel Roll-Up Sandwich,
    110–11
Pumpkin-Pecan Bread, 62
pumpkin seeds, in Chewy Coun-
    try Bread with Seeds, 116
pushcart breads, 174–82
    Bagel and Pretzel Dough, Basic,
       175

pushcart breads (*continued*)
 Butter-Dipped Pretzels, 180
 Chewy New York–Style
  Bagels, Basic, 176–77
 German–Style Pretzels, Real,
  178–79
 Potato Knishes, 181–82

Raised Doughnuts and Doughnut
  Holes, 138–39
raisin(s):
 -Banana Oat Bread, 89–90
 Challah, 66
 -Cinnamon Bagels, 177
 -Cinnamon Bread, 42
 -Cinnamon Whole-Wheat
  Loaf, 86
 Cornmeal Honey Loaf, 43
 Pandoro, 78–79
 Sticky Buns, 132–33
Rand Youth Poll, 19
Real Farmhouse Potato Bread,
  39–40
Red Star Yeast and Products, 198
Regal Ware, 198
rice flour, in Dutch-Crunch Din-
  ner Rolls, 125–26
ricotta cheese, in White Pizza, 155
rising, 29, 30
 excessive, 194
 insufficient, 193–94
Robin Hood Multifoods, 198
rolls:
 Suizos, 76–77
 see also bun(s); dinner rolls
Roll-Up Sandwich, Pumpernickel,
  110–11
Rosemary-and-Black-Olive Bread,
  115
 as *Banneton,* 121–22
 as French Bread (*Baguettes*),
  119–20
 as *Partybrot,* 123–24
Russian Black Bread, 108–9
rye breads, 101–11
 Good Old New York Deli, 102

Pumpernickel Roll-Up Sand-
  wich, 110–11
 Russian Black, 108–9
 St. Paddy's Day, 105
 Sourdough, Old Milwaukee,
  107
 Sour Starter for, 106
 Swedish *Limpa,* 103–4
rye flour, 23
 adding to white-flour breads,
  37
 Multigrain Bread, 92

Sage-and-Onion *Focaccia,* 168–69
St. Paddy's Day Rye, 105
St. Paddy's Day Shamrocks, 149
Salad, *Panzanella,* 190
Salmorejo, 191
salsa, in South-of-the-Border
  Pizza, 156
salt, 26, 27
 measuring, 27
 -Rising Bread, 50
 -Rising Bread Starter, 49
Salton, 198
Sandwich, Pumpernickel Roll-Up,
  110-11
Sanyo, 198
sausage, in Chicago Deep-Dish
  Pizza, 157–58
savory:
 Butterhorns, 97–98
 Egg Bread, 55–56
scallions:
 Deep-Dish Taco Bake, 159–60
 South-of-the-Border Pizza, 156
Scandinavian breads:
 Danish *Kringle,* 134–35
 Swedish *Limpa* Rye, 103–4
seeds:
 Chewy Country Bread with,
  116
 see also specific seeds
Semolina Bread with Toasted
  Sesame Seeds, 114
 as *Banneton,* 121–22

as French Bread (*Baguettes*),
  119–20
 as *Partybrot,* 123–24
semolina flour, 23
sesame seeds:
 Aladdin's Bread, 172–73
 Chewy Country Bread with
  Seeds, 116
 Golden Wheat Bread with, 86
 Savory Butterhorns, 97–98
 Savory Egg Bread with, 56
 Toasted, Semolina Bread with,
  114
7 UP, in Sweet Bread, 59–60
Shamrocks, St. Paddy's Day, 149
shortening, 26
 measuring, 28
Soup, *Salmorejo,* 191
sourdough:
 Rye Bread, Old Milwaukee,
  107
 Rye Sour Starter for, 106
 Starter, 47
 White Bread, 48
South-of-the-Border Pizza, 156
 Crust, 152
Spanish fare:
 Salmorejo, 191
 Suizos, 76–77
spices:
 adding to bread machine, 27
 measuring, 27
Spinach and Mozzarella Filling,
  for Garlic Knots, 161–63
starters:
 Rye Sour, 106
 Salt-Rising Bread, 49
 Sourdough, 47
Steamed Barbecued-Pork Buns,
  52
Sticky Buns, 132–33
sticky dough, troubleshooting tips
  for, 192–93
Stollen, Christmas, 140–41
storing bread and dough, 31
Strata, 188

sugar, 26–27
measuring, 27
substituting honey for, 37
Suizos, 76–77
Sunbeam, 198
Swedish *Limpa* Rye, 103–4
sweet breads:
Almond-and-Cherry, 65
Apple-Chunk and Walnut Pull-
Apart, 82
Butterhorns, 97–98
Chocolate-Crumb Pull-Apart,
Funny as a Monkey, 81
Christmas, 60
Lemon Poppy-Seed Loaf,
Glazed, 63–64
Orange-Cranberry-Walnut
Loaf, 61
Pandoro, 78–79
Pull-Apart Bubble Bread
Dough, Basic, 80
Pumpkin-Pecan, 62
Suizos, 76–77
Sweet Bread, 59–60
Tropical Hawaiian Bubble, 83
see also pastry(ies)
sweeteners, 26–27
sticky, measuring, 27–28
Swiss cheese, in Pumpernickel
Roll-Up Sandwich, 110–11

taco:
Bake, Deep-Dish, 159–60
seasonings, in South-of-the-
Border Pizza Crust, 152
Toast, Cinnamon, 184
Toastmaster, 198
tomato(es):
-and-Basil Bread, 117
as *Banneton,* 121–22
as French Bread (*Baguettes*),
119–20
as *Partybrot,* 123–24
and Bread, 189
-and-Cheese Pie, Classic,
153–54

Deep-Dish Taco Bake, 159–
60
Panzanella, 190
Salmorejo, 191
Tropical Hawaiian Bubble Bread,
83
troubleshooting, 32, 192–96
collapsed bread, 194–95
crust problems, 195–96
dried fruits and nuts, 196
excessive rising, 194
insufficient rising, 193–94
kneading problems, 192
sticky dough, 192–93
underbaked bread, 195

unbleached flour, 22
undercooked bread, 195

Valentine Hearts, 148
vegetable oil, 26
Veggie Buns, Buddha's Delightful,
53

walnut(s):
and Apple-Chunk Pull-Apart
Bread, 82
-Apple Wheat Bread, 94
Black-Olive-and-Rosemary
Bread with, 115
-Brownie Bread, Chocolatey, 41
Cinnamon-Raisin Bread with,
42
Old-Fashioned Oat Bread with,
46
-Orange-Cranberry Loaf, 61
Sticky Buns, 132–33
Sweet Butterhorns, 97–98
Toasted-, -and-Pesto Bread,
118
Whole-Wheat Date-Nut Bread,
95
water, 25, 26
measuring, 28
weight equivalents, 28
Welbilt, 198

West Bend, 198
wheat breads:
Apple-Walnut, 94
Golden, 85–86
see also whole-wheat
(graham) flour
Wheat-Flake Potato Bread, 87–88
wheat germ, adding to white-flour
breads, 37
white bread flour, 22–23, 35
white breads, 35–53
adding rye flour to, 37
adding wheat germ to, 37
Banneton, 121–22
Buddha's Delightful Veggie
Buns, 53
Buttermilk, Old-Fashioned,
38
Chinese Bun Dough, Basic,
51
Chocolatey Walnut-Brownie,
41
Cinnamon-Raisin, 42
Cornmeal Honey Loaf, 43
Dutch-Crunch Dinner Rolls,
125–26
European, Basic, 113
French (*Baguettes*), 119–20
Homey, 36–37
Irish Freckle, 44
Oat, Old-Fashioned, 45–46
Partybrot, 123–24
Pesto-and-Toasted Walnut,
118
Potato, Real Farmhouse, 39–40
Salt-Rising, 50
Salt-Rising Bread Starter, 49
Semolina, with Toasted Sesame
Seeds, 114
Sourdough, 48
Sourdough Starter, 47
Steamed Barbecued-Pork Buns,
52
Tomato-and-Basil, 117
White Pizza, 155
White-Westinghouse, 198

whole-grain breads, 84–100
  Apple-Walnut Wheat, 94
  Banana-Raisin Oat, 89–90
  Golden Wheat, 85–86
  Multigrain, 92
  100 Percent Whole-Wheat,
    93
  PBJ (Peanut-Butter-and-Jelly),
    91
  Wheat-Flake Potato, 87–88
  Whole-Wheat-and-Honey
    Bagels, 177
  Whole-Wheat Date-Nut, 95
  Whole-Wheat Raisin-Cinna-
    mon Loaf, 86
  see also rye breads; whole-wheat
    pastry(ies)
whole-wheat (graham) flour,
  22–23

Apple-Walnut Wheat Bread, 94
Banana-Raisin Oat Bread,
  89–90
Black-Olive-and-Rosemary
  Bread, 115
Golden Wheat Bread, 85–86
Multigrain Bread, 92
100 Percent Whole-Wheat
  Bread, 93
PBJ (Peanut-Butter-and-Jelly)
  Bread, 91
Wheat-Flake Potato Bread,
  87–88
Whole-Wheat-and-Honey
  Bagels, 177
Whole-Wheat Date-Nut Bread,
  95
Whole-Wheat Pizza Crust,
  152

whole-wheat pastry(ies):
  Coconut-Pecan Coffee Cake,
    99–100
  Dough, Basic, 96
  Sweet or Savory Butterhorns,
    97–98

yeast, 23–25
  checking activity of, 24–25
  fermentation process and,
    23–24, 25, 26, 27
  gluten and, 22
  measuring, 27
  sugar and salt and, 26
  and temperature of ingredients,
    25, 26, 28
  types of, 24

Zojirushi, 198